It has been a privilege to get to know Rhéa over the years and to be a recipient of her loving heart. Through all Rhéa's life challenges, she has remained generous and giving, passionate for God, contending for her country, loving her family and friends, and with a heart for those who are yet to know God.

Rhéa's book is insightful, motivating, thought-provoking, and sprinkled with joy. It reveals her faith, belief, and encourages others that they can overcome too. The best part is her story isn't finished yet!

Dustine Kinsella
Artist; Ordained Minister
Certified Mental Health Coach
www.DustineArt.com

Rhéa's stories take you on an adventure with her. You feel like you're journeying right there with her through her ups and downs. On this journey with her, you will experience the God of divine intervention, divine encounters, and divine miracles. You will sense and feel God's hand of favour over Rhéa's life, and you will be encouraged by her gift of faith. Rhéa truly is an overcomer, and she has a brilliant way of seeing and experiencing God's nature through the people she meets on life's journey. I encourage you to take this journey with her and read *Learning to Fly with a*

Broken Wing. You will be encouraged and inspired by the God who saves, by the God who heals, by the God who brings life.

Jeanette Sthamann
Prophetic Artist; Wife and Mother
Brushed by The Spirit
www.brushedbythespirit.com

Rhéa's book is thought provoking, inspirational, and has insightful accounts of God showing up in significant moments and situations. Grab a cup of tea or coffee and go on an easy-to-read-through journey with Rhéa as she takes you on her God journeys of life.

Margaret McDermott
Life Coach and Mentor
Author of *Be Still and Know,*
Life Beyond Stress, and
Where Am I Going and How Do I Get There

Rhéa has written this book on the reality of God's interaction and intent to be very real and present in our lives. For those who have ever asked the question "Where is God?", this is a must-read account—life-altering and real. Thanks, Rhéa, for being vulnerable and sharing your experiences.

Petrina Gratton
Friend and Fellow Lover of Jesus

Learning to Fly with a Broken Wing is a book written like a candid conversation with a friend, best consumed with coffee. Rhéa shares her life and faith journey in word snapshots, narrating her experiences with poignancy and humour in equal measure. The reader will be uplifted and encouraged to discover the goodness of God amid life's challenges.

Sonja Zacharias
Artist and Art Instructor

LEARNING TO FLY
with a
BROKEN WING

God Encounters Along The Way

RHEA DALLAIRE

Learning to Fly with a Broken Wing: God Encounters Along the Way
By Rhéa Dallaire
Copyright © 2021 Lion's Roar Publishing

Published by Lion's Roar Publishing
Email: rhea@thelionsroars.com

Cover Design & Layout by: ChristianAuthorsGetPaid.com

DISCLAIMER:

This collection of stories has had limited editing done and been left relatively untouched and unfiltered. It is strictly from the author's point of view as she wrote it and is presented the way she received it.

Furthermore, the author has designed the information of this book around her own experiences, encounters, thoughts, and insights. Although the author speaks from her heart and personal experience, she disclaims any liability, loss, or risk incurred by individuals reading or acting on the information presented to them in this book. The author believes the encouragement and insights given here to be sound, but readers cannot hold the author, publisher, or any of their agents responsible for either the actions they take or the results of those actions.

Printed in the United States of America

ISBN: 978-1-7777506-0-2

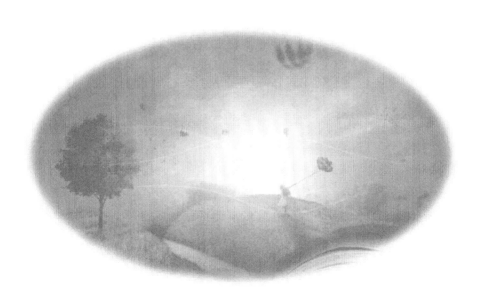

Dedication

I dedicate this book to

THE TRINITY

for loving me

and to my good friend

EMMANUEL.

He taught me humility

and showed me much kindness,

which is one of God's greatest

currencies upon the earth.

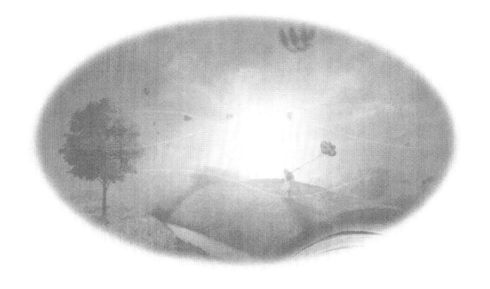

Acknowledgements

First of all, thank you to the members of the Trinity, who have relentlessly pursued me, loved on me, and encouraged me to follow God's design for my life. Somehow, they have fashioned beauty out of ashes. I am forever grateful for their never-ending love and their keeping power in preserving my life for such a time as this.

To Miss Leita Ritch... You are an unsung hero upon this earth! You adopted me and my family in friendship and through intercession over 30 years ago. How do I adequately thank you for all the sleepless nights you had bringing us before the Throne? I have told many that I believe you will have one of the largest mansions in Heaven because you are always "sending up lumber" through your prayers and selfless life. Plus, there have been all the wonderful miracles through your service to the Lord. You and Jesus raised a pilot from the dead in the Amazon jungle. When you baked a loaf or casserole, many got healed upon partaking of it. You are one of my heroes upon the earth for your example of how to give your life away for the sake of the Kingdom.

A special thanks goes out to my family and all the faithful friends and intercessors who have stood by me all these years. Some have prayed for and walked with me over decades. Many of your prayers literally saved my life on many occasions. I love you all!

There are those of you who have also prayed for this book and its finish line, walking with me in the journey of writing. I do not take this for granted. The stories contained here will be as fruit to your heavenly account. You know who you are. I pray that all your cups run over with His goodness for what you have sowed into my life and this book, for Heaven knows your names.

To the tireless labourers who have worked directly on this book... What can I say except "mucho grande thank you" and another big "THANK YOU" for pushing me out of my comfort zone to get this out. This would never have been possible without all of your help. Blessings to all of you!

I am so thankful for all my destiny helpers!

Table of Contents

1 ..... Introduction

3 ..... Born in a Crowd

5 ..... Banana Box Baby

7 ..... Losing the Love of My Life

9 ..... Inside My Four-Year-Old Head's Recollections

11 ..... Funeral Day

13 ..... The Accident

15 ..... "You will not have my kids or my land!"

17 ..... My Passion for the Arts and Teaching Emerges in Childhood

19 ..... God's Gift of Writing

21 ..... I can drive that...without a license!

25 ..... Transferred to Sherwood Park

27 ..... God Saves My Dying Son

31 ..... Miraculous Healing from Epilepsy

33 ..... Jesus Heals My Son of Epilepsy

35 ..... Oil Field "Boom, Bust, and Transfer"

41 ..... The Holy Ghost Speaks: "My Nephew" – Suicide

45 ..... "80-Year-Old Plumber"

51	..... God's Sense of "Ha"
55	..... "I've got rivers of Living Water, and I've got a good-looking liver."
61	..... Joy for a Whole Year
63	..... House Fire
67	..... God Knows when You Are in the Dump
71	..... Shopping for His Heart
73	..... A Lesson Learned from the Fire
77	..... Face-to-Face Encounter
79	..... Healed of Insomnia
81	..... A United Effort
83	..... Totem Poles and the Inuit
85	..... Gold Dust
87	..... Back to the Inuit
89	..... Lightning Bolts and Fireballs
93	..... Commanding Tornadoes to Cease
95	..... Jesus at Tim Horton's
99	..... Lost in a McDonald's Parking Lot (Seriously!)
101	..... 300 Prodigals Come Home
105	..... "God says go! God says go!"
107	..... The Agenda Behind the Agenda
109	..... Bridal Shop Encounters

111   ..... A Bride Named Trinity

113   ..... A Bride Called Faith

115   ..... Chocolate Angel

119   ..... "God, I live in a barn."

123   ..... From Garden of Weedin' to Garden of Eden

127   ..... Moving to Kelowna

131   ..... Jesus at a Soup Kitchen

135   ..... The Greatest Invitation

137   ..... Nation Quakers

141   ..... Three Ambulance Rides in a Decade

151   ..... God Wants Out of the Box

155   ..... Caught in a Canadian Court System

159   ..... Hit by a Mack Truck

163   ..... Broken-Down Jesus Girl Touches the Heart of a King

169   ..... "Ransomed Warrior"

171   ..... Summary

Introduction

This book is a testimony of life's ups and downs. The writing of this book was not some great thought or desire of yours truly. For you see, I believe the Trinity had pre-thought the idea before I was born. I can perhaps hear their conversation now. They may have been saying:

> "Watch this one! She doesn't know it yet, but she will have to overcome much at an early age. She doesn't know it yet, but she was created to overcome. As she overcomes pain, adversity, tragedy, and loss after loss, we will use this one to bring hope to others. In fact, she will help motivate others to believe us to overcome. For if they see she has overcome a multitude of very difficult circumstances, it shall give others courage of heart. They will then see that we, the Godhead, shall be with them to help them overcome."

I have received eleven prophecies that I was to write. Many of the folks who prophesied over me did not know each other.

The eighth one was from my pastor. When he stopped preaching mid-service and prophesied that, I went to him after the service. "What would I write about?" I asked him.

He said, "You will write about overcoming as you have had to overcome so much."

The eleventh prophecy came through a woman named Theresa. I had never met her, and she came and stood beside me in a conference line up. We were waiting for prophetic ministry. She suddenly turned to me and said, "Are you called to write?" She continued, "You are called to write, and you need to write because you have fresh stories for the Body of Christ, and we need to hear your stories."

Well, that put the fear of the Lord in me. I knew I could not hold back. Shortly after, I began to write in obedience to the Holy Spirit.

Woven throughout these testimonies and encounters, you will see the life encouragement and lessons the Lord taught me along the way. You will find no eloquent speech in these pages. My simple hope is that you, the reader, will be encouraged. If God did it for me, He will do it for you. Who knows, perhaps you will be inspired to grab a pen and begin to write your stories out too.

Blessings!

Rhéa Hope

Born in a Crowd

While I am not particularly a crowd person, I must admit I was brought into this world in a crowd. I am the 11th child of 12. On my mother's side of the family, I have 88 first cousins. Need more proof of it being a crowd? I think not. It made up for my father's side as most of them had died at young ages from sickness, so not a lot of immediate relatives there.

My parents were going to name me Rebekah, Ramona, or Rhéa. My mother said my father insisted it had to be Rhéa.

My mother was warned by her doctor after her 5th child that she should not have any more children, or she could die. Well, being from a Roman Catholic faith, birth control was not an option. We lived in northern Canada. We had cold winters; hence, many children were born there. You can imagine all the fear my mother had through having each successive child. I had, in the womb, inherited that fear and had to overcome it and many other fears.

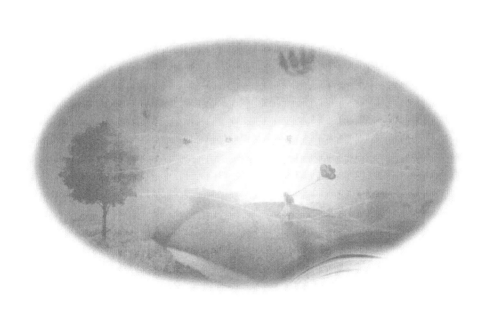

Banana Box Baby

Don't despise the day of small beginnings. (See Zechariah 4:10)

Recently, while having a conversation with one of my sisters, she shared something with me. I had never known about this prior to our conversation about my infant years.

When I was born, our family was poor, and times were hard. My brother, who was a year and a half older than me, was very sick with a very rare condition called Bright's disease. I haven't heard much of it before or since. All I know is that he was very sick.

My mother was often on a train to visit him in Edmonton. I guess he got the crib when he came home.

So, when my sister asked me, "Rhéa, do you know what your bed was when you were a baby?" I didn't know. I assumed I had a crib too. She said, "No, your bed was a banana box."

She said my mother went to the store and got a large banana box and made a bed for me in there. My sister recalled being about 14 years old at the time and looking into the box to see me. She said Mom put the box on the freezer so that she could watch me as she cooked. My sister always felt sad for me as she peeked over the edge of my banana box cradle.

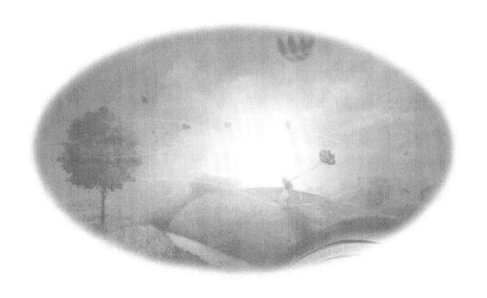

Losing the Love of My Life

On October 31, 1969—Halloween night—Death came to visit our house. I recall standing in the kitchen that morning. My parents were fighting. I remember loud voices yelling back and forth. My mother didn't want my father going somewhere. He kept saying, "I'm going!" On and on that went. I was 4 years old. That's all I remember from that morning.

The next morning, I was in the barn with all my siblings. They were milking cows. I was likely playing with the kittens of which we always had an ample supply. My furry, fluffy world was about to change. I was soon to find out something about my wonderful, loving father.

He taught his 11 remaining children to kneel at a chair on the kitchen floor to pray for one hour every night. We formed a circle with the chairs, and even if you were two or three years old, you had to pray or participate in the family prayer time.

My "Knight in Shining Armour" would no longer take me in his lap each night after he had tidied up from chores.

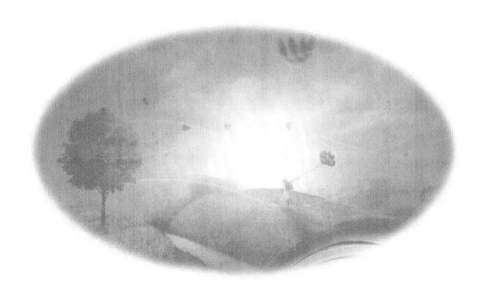

Inside My Four-Year-Old Head's Recollections

Out of nowhere appeared a police car and our parish priest. I do not recall who came to the barn, but I did take notice that all my siblings were weeping and weeping with heads hanging down, carrying their milk pails to the house from the barn.

We had a cream separator in our front porch. Here we separated the cream from the milk. My mother sold the cream to help support the farm.

I remember going to stand by my father's nice, black car. I don't know why I did that, but at that moment, somehow, I must have felt that I would be close to him...somehow.

In the following days, I know I got some new clothes, and we got big wreaths at the house. I still did not know what was happening but probably thought that it was fun. Little did my four-year-old mind know that it was all for the funeral.

Funeral. Wow! A Big Word. I did not have a clue what that was or why we would be going to one. I still was not sure what all the fuss was about.

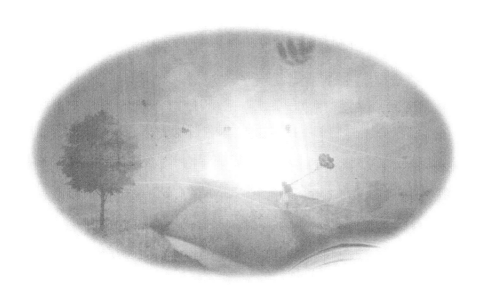

Funeral Day

We were sitting in church, which was not unusual as we always went to church. The one thing I couldn't figure out was why my father was sleeping in a black box on the stage. He always loved to take a nap, but why here, why now, and why in that elevated black box?

I was sitting next to my mother. I asked her if I could go and give my dad a kiss. She shook her head and said, "No." I didn't get it...he was only asleep.

I turned and saw all my big brothers sitting behind me, and they were all weeping and weeping. I had never seen them cry. I loved my brothers, and it hurt my heart to see them cry. I couldn't figure out why they would have had anything to cry about?

By the time the funeral came, my dad had been dead for seven days. The funeral home had him covered in a lot of formaldehyde and makeup because he was so mangled from the accident, and his body was starting to leak.

My eldest brother had been working in a city funeral home, but he had to come home and identify my dad. He never could work in a funeral home after that.

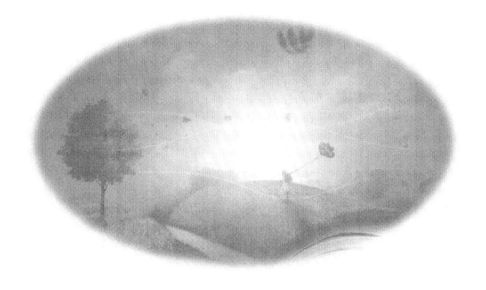

The Accident

My father had gone out on that cold Halloween night to buy a tractor. My mom's youngest brother, my uncle, went with him. (I got the whole story from my uncle almost 40 some years later when I called to wish him a happy birthday. He and I share the same birthday.)

I had heard some stories over the years that Dad had been killed by drunk drivers who were from the same area where we lived. Here is my uncle's version given when I called and thanked him for being there with my dad that night...

He shared that they had made a deal to take turns riding the tractor and driving the van home. My dad insisted on driving the tractor. He was likely proud of his new purchase and how he could provide for his family. Anyway, a drunk driver hit him.

There was no cab on that tractor. My father lay dying on the highway. There were no cell phones, so my uncle had to run to a farmer nearby and get help.

When the police got there, they opened the truck door of the drunken men. These men did not realize what had transpired and said, "We are outta beer."

My uncle said he dreaded going to our farmhouse at 3:00 a.m. to tell my mom that she had no more husband and that we had no father. He had carried this trauma with him for all those years. He said, "Rhéa," as he wept, "I always wondered why I got to live when I had no kids, but your dad had 12 kids, and he died." I thanked him and told him that night wasn't his fault. We all turned out well, and God had a plan.

Through my life, he and my aunt would always look at me tenderly, and now I knew why.

"You will not have my kids or my land!"

My poor maman (as we called her in French) had so many children. At times, she probably didn't know what to do...but she never let on to us. She was the hardest working woman I have met in my whole life. She got her heavenly wings in February 2015. I'm sure her crown is full of many jewels plus many more for her longsuffering and very hard work.

Her parents had 17 children. Yup, we were French Catholic. Mom was the second born, and she helped raise most of her siblings due to her mother always having more children. Then, Mom and Dad had 12 of us. One baby girl died due to being born in the back seat of a car on a cold November night. She was considered a blue baby and died 24 hours later.

So, I have a sister named Carmen who I will be reunited with in Heaven. I have always marveled at that tiny baby headstone near my father's gravesite. The name Carmen means "Garden Song". She never got to sing her song. Maybe, I will help sing it for her.

Apparently, when my father died, Social Services came to visit my mother, telling her that they could help her if she would simply give them some of her children and some land. The Lion of the Tribe of Judah rose up in my momma, and she said, "You will not have my kids or my land!"

She would *not* let our family be split up! She worked like a dog to keep us all together and to keep the farm. My older brother stayed back for a while after he graduated high school to help my mother keep the farm.

You know, sometimes you just gotta rise up and be tenacious like my momma was. You gotta say, "Devil, you are not gonna have my kids or my land (or my health, etc.)!" Tell him so and say it like you mean it. Tell him to get outta your way!

My Passion for the Arts and Teaching Emerges in Childhood

As an artist, I enjoy the process of creating. It's a God-given gift and desire. As a child, it began with paper, pencils, and a box of Crayola crayons. I loved everything about that box—the bright colour orange, the rainbow of assorted colours inside, and yes, even the smell of those wax crayons. It was exhilarating to think of all the masterpieces I could create.

If I were told to colour inside the lines by a well-meaning art teacher, I would colour outside the lines. That was proof of a bit of a rebel inside me...or maybe it was just that I was a child who knew there was more living to be done beyond walls and borders. Besides, why miss out on all the fun?

My adventures also took me to mixed media at an early age. I would glue popcorn, beans, rocks, yarn, and string to anything I could find.

I wanted to act too. My sister and I would put striped beach towels on our heads while looking at the TV and saying, "I'm her," or "No, I'm her," while watching the actresses. We also played "Miss Canada Pageant" with our older sister using my mother's housecoat and high heels. We would take the wooden orange crates and stack them up. One stack had three crates, next to it were two crates, and then one stack had one crate. The eldest of the contestants in our homemade show always won "Miss Canada" and got to stand on the three crates. My other sister always won first runner-up and got to stand on the two crates. Somehow, I always got the one crate and was crowned second runner-up.

My teaching gift was discovered by all my dolls and bears. They were the ones who, whether they liked it or not, had to endure sitting in my brother's red wagon or being propped up on the floor while I taught them everything that I had learned that day in school. My stepfather built me a large blackboard, and I'm sure I almost wore it out.

God's Gift of Writing

While in the fifth grade, the school I was attending held a writing competition for the grade 4, 5, and 6 students. The contest subject was: "What would you do if you were elected the Elementary School Coordinator?" Basically, how would we run the school?

The winner would get to be the Elementary School Coordinator for one day. They would get to stroll the hallways, walk into each class to observe and give input, and have coffee and lunch breaks with all the elementary teachers, staff, and the school principal. Well, much to my surprise, out of all the grade 4, 5, and 6 students, my essay and writing won that contest!

Before I knew it, the day came for me to run that elementary school. I remember thinking, *"Who me?"* but I did settle into those shoes quite quickly when I learned that all those teachers wanted to glean from my young mind and counsel. They actually listened, smiled, and, I think, enjoyed it as much as I did. A certain amount of pride came from thinking: *"Wow, I think I could do this teaching thing."* My peers did not seem jealous but actually celebrated with me winning and didn't mind my seniority for the day.

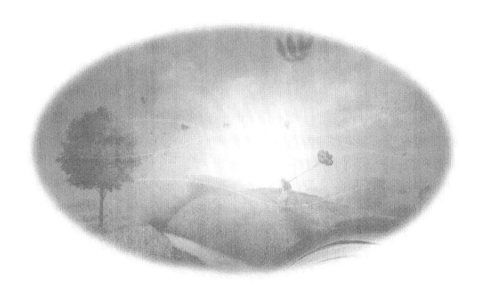

I can drive that...
without a license!

When I was 15, my parents moved to my stepfather's farm. My stepfather wanted to teach me how to drive. We had triangle-stacked hay stooks in the field. They were made of several hay bales and looked quite pretty I thought. Dad would take the half-ton truck out there, and then put me in the driver's seat. It was a standard as was the tractor I also drove.

Many times, I recall almost giving both of us whiplash on both of those vehicles while learning to drive them. Frustrated and embarrassed that Dad did not trust me to take the truck on the road, I stewed. Instead, he made me go around the stooks in that field and then try to back up in between them. Seriously? I thought it was dumb!

One day, I asked him why he didn't ever let me drive on the road. He said, "If you hit those bales, you won't hurt anyone." I got it, okay. But the backing up part still bugged me.

Finally, one day, I had totally had it backing up. I belted out, "Dad, I'm not backing up anymore! That's it!"

He was quiet, and then he said, "How do you figure that out?"

I simply and matter-of-factly stated, "Well, from now on and for the rest of my life, I'm always gonna park where I can drive in and then drive straight out again."

He laughed. And he remembered this for years right up until his deathbed.

Somehow, it was just like God was saying, "Listen here, sweetheart, the way I see it, you will have to eat humble pie many times in your life, but I'll let you rant and rave till you back up again." Oh, the wisdom of parents!

Little did I know how handy my field driving lessons from my dad would be. You see, that summer I was chosen to travel across Canada to represent the National Farmers Union for our whole region. Dad was the president, and all the farmers asked about sending me. They all loved me and thought I would be a prime candidate.

When Dad approached me, I was shocked. Again, who me? But before I knew it, I was with 45 other high school students from Western Canada travelling east by either Greyhound or plane across Canada to Detroit and Chicago.

I stayed for 2 weeks on a potato farm in New Brunswick. I was fortunate to stay there with a lovely young couple whose daughter's name was Rhéa also. One day, they said we were gonna ride in a spray plane. The spray planes sprayed the farmer's potato crops.

Thankfully, my dear girlfriend on the trip was staying a quarter mile from the farm. She was invited also. Off we went to the field and boarded the plane.

I loved it! The plane went high and then low, to and fro, spraying as it did. I totally loved it. It was really quite beautiful from above it all. It was not that I liked the sprays, but for a 15-year-old farm girl, this was a blast. We sure didn't get to do this back home.

Upon landing, several farmers and men lined up all the larger, cargo potato trucks. They were getting ready to depart when one of them said, "We are short one driver." They looked around puzzled.

Out of my mouth and before I could think, I piped up, "I can do that."

Surprised, they all looked at me—a little, blond, blue-eyed farm girl from the West. I must have looked confident as they did not do a lot of questioning before handing me some keys. The deal was on, and I would follow this caravan of potato trucks with their tall, wooden boxes.

I don't recall being nervous. Somehow, I had convinced myself I could just do it. Right? Well, about a mile or so down the road, I began to ask my girlfriend how I was to gear down and get this truck onto the long, winding driveway off the highway. She had a bit of experience, and so did I. So, I figured that two heads were better than one.

For that first mile, we laughed with pride that they had trusted us. Neither one of us had a license, and now we were going down the highway.

All was well 'til we thought about that turnoff. All I knew about highway driving was to simply stay on the right side of that yellow line and then stay between the lines.

To this day, I do not know how we got that truck up that difficult driveway without tipping the whole truck over into the ditch. We musta had big angels or God alerted all of Heaven to watch and pray. The truck got there safely, and those farmers were proud.

When I got home and told my dad, he said, "You did WHAT?"

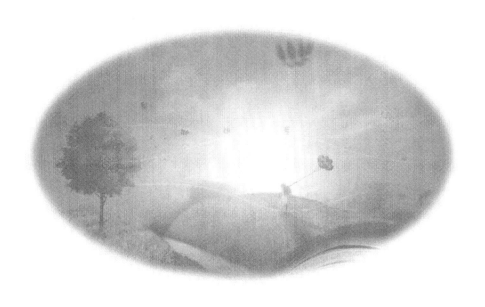

Transferred to Sherwood Park

I finished high school in 1982 and got married in 1985. In the summer of 1987, our family got transferred to another city—Sherwood Park, Alberta. My husband was in the oil patch, and we had a saying, "Such is the life of an oil patch wife."

Oil companies don't care a lot about families, and often these families have to relocate over and over again. We had a house in a northern Alberta town. We rented that out to a couple of nurses and headed to Sherwood Park.

Crazy thing was, I had to leave all my support system, family, and friends to go to a city where I knew no one. The company, who paid for our move, then proceeded to send my husband *back* to that town (where we had family, friends, and a house that we rented out). Then, he had to live in a hotel 5 days a week. Then, he would be home on weekends.

I tried to make the best of it, but it was hard. Now, I had other women renting my home, I was away from family and friends, and the oil company had moved us there and sent him back. Crazy making for sure!

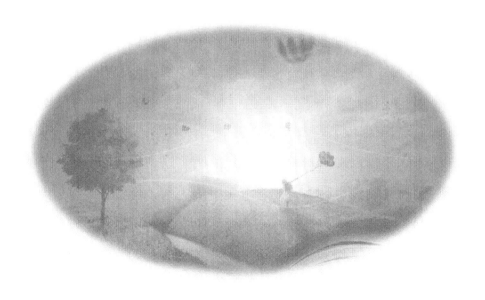

God Saves My Dying Son

The day we arrived in Sherwood Park, the movers came, unloaded, helped set up beds, and left. We unpacked the kitchen and got that set up first.

Around 9:00 at night, our son, Cody[1], who was three years old, came up to me in the master bedroom. I was starting to go through boxes there. He asked if he could have a candy. I said, "What candy?"

He took me to the kitchen and showed me a candy in a wrapper in the bottom of a box. You see, paid movers are supposed to pack everything they find. They will even pack your keys, your last pair of shoes if you don't set those aside, etc. So, someone had found a candy in a drawer or cupboard and threw it in a box. Well, my son was excited.

I said, "No."

He persisted and even said, "Mom, I'll brush my teeth." I could not resist that intelligence and cuteness.

So, he put the candy in his mouth and proceeded to walk into the living room. I heard a voice inside of me saying persistently, "Follow him." It felt strangely strong, and I knew I needed to obey for some reason.

He walked to a certain point and turned around. When he turned around, I could only see the white of his eyes. His eyes

---

[1] Name changed to protect privacy

had rolled back, and the candy was on the edge of his tongue as his tongue stuck out of his mouth. He looked numb or stunned.

I began to call his name over and over. He couldn't hear me. He couldn't respond. I knew he was in Big Trouble. I yelled for my husband to come. I gently grabbed Cody's shoulders and yelled out his name several times, over and over. Nothing.

The next thing I knew, my husband had picked up our son. I opened the back door, and we ran for help. When I opened the backyard gate, Cody went limp in his father's arms and started turning blue.

Here we were, two young parents with a young boy in a new city, knowing no one except our next-door neighbour, who for some reason had mentioned when we rented the house that the brick-red strip mall behind the house had a 24-hour emergency clinic if we needed one. Now, we were running like madmen in hopes that somebody could help us save this child.

After we left the backyard gate, I started crying and screaming, "Somebody help me! My baby is dying!" Over and over, I said this. Cody's body was turning blue. We had to run a long way 'til we could finally see a sign that read "Medical Clinic".

There were two men outside the clinic. They were doctors who had just locked up the clinic doors. That was miraculous due to the fact that the clinic was no longer a 24-hour clinic but a 9-5 clinic. It had changed its hours since our landlord had raised his children. These two doctors (or angels) had been doing karate, and the one fellow had injured his thumb. They had come back to the clinic to bandage him up. We didn't know who they were from Adam.

My son was set on the sidewalk. The one doctor started mouth-to-mouth resuscitation and digging in his throat. The other doctor was fighting to get the clinic door open. I was still hysterically crying and saying, "Somebody help me! My baby is dying!"

All of a sudden, I felt this massive hug from behind as I threw my hands in the air. A bright triangle of light came over us. The minute that happened, Cody started to cry. I knew that if a choking victim could make a sound, they would often be okay.

The hug from behind me was an elderly woman who lived in the house beside us. She had had her window open, heard the yelling, saw us running, and followed us.

The doctor then got the clinic door open. The other doctor carried Cody in. They laid him on a table. He was crying, but they seemed relieved and said he was gonna be okay.

All I kept saying was, "That was God. That was God."

We went home, and a friend called from Edmonton. I told her what had happened, and they drove out. I remember crying by my son's bed 'til midnight that night, and all I could say over and over was, "That was God. That was God." I told my husband, "I don't know where He is, but I'm gonna find Him."

The next morning at 10:00 a.m., there was a knock on the door. It was one of the doctors. He had come to check on Cody. He checked him and saw that he was fine. He said that, for the time he was out, he should have had major brain damage, but he didn't. He was in awe. He said, "You do know that was a miracle as there was nothing we could do?"

I knew that no one but God had saved my son's life.

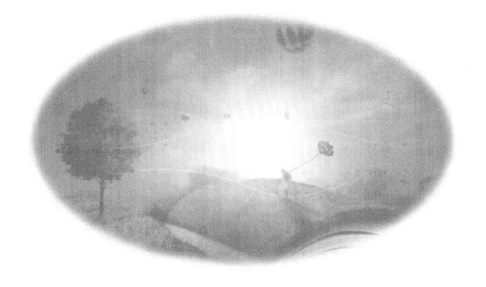

Miraculous Healing from Epilepsy

About a month to 6 weeks later, this same child had something funny happen at the breakfast table. We were sitting eating our breakfast, and he said, "I saw the cat...(then he missed a long, blank space of time and proceeded to finish his sentence)...run across the road."

When he finished, I wondered what had happened but then dismissed it. The problem was, this type of long pause with eyes rolled back in the middle of a sentence happened again.

The second time it happened, I asked him why he was doing that. He said, "Doing what?" This was when I knew that something unusual was happening.

I booked him in to see a doctor who then referred us to a neurologist at the University Hospital in Edmonton. I spent three years in that office with Cody as they had to monitor him a lot. He had epilepsy. Doctors weren't sure if it was due to him almost dying at birth due to a very difficult delivery and the use of high forceps or his choking incident. They put him on the drug Phenobarbital.

He was so drugged it was like having 10 kids in one child's earth suit. Very difficult times and much crying happened in those years. That drug was for adults and so bad that they finally took it off the market years later.

31

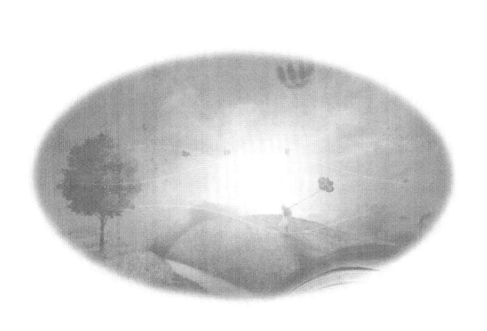

Jesus Heals My Son
of Epilepsy

Cody had 20 – 30 petit mal seizures. Not the drop seizure but bad enough.

A friend of mine was taking me to a Bible study, and at this Bible study, they always talked of Jesus. In fact, to this day, I have never seen a group like this. They were all Catholics who had experienced "Renewal."

When you mentioned the name Jesus, they all began to weep. I mean the whole room, for the whole time. I was raised Catholic, but even I knew they were different. I mean, they *knew* Him, like *really knew* Him, not like a faraway God but as a person.

I thought I should ask this group to come to my house for an evening to host their event. I thought, *"Surely, they won't be weeping here."* But sure enough, the same thing happened.

At the end of the evening, they recommended I read the book of Revelation. I started promptly. I began to trust in this God they knew. I mean, there was no way anyone on earth could manufacture those kinds of tears. You would only cry that much for one you loved or one you knew loved you. I wasn't sure how all this worked, but I was beginning to see God as a real person.

One day as I stood over the kitchen sink with the bottle of epilepsy medicine for Cody in one hand and a spoon in the other,

I said to my husband, "If the Lord saved his life, can't He heal him?"

I dropped the spoon full of medicine in the sink. He never had another seizure again—he was totally healed of a three-year nightmare called epilepsy.

God was getting my attention. My hunger for more of this God was becoming more of a reality to me.

Oil Field "Boom, Bust, and Transfer"

In the fall of that year, my husband got laid off. The boom of the oil patch had now burst. People were losing jobs. Families had to relocate to where the new jobs were, and again, family life was disrupted.

We had a huge 3000 sq. ft. Cape Cod style home on an acreage three miles from town. I loved that place! It was close enough yet far enough away from everything.

We didn't know what to do. We had three mouths to feed, a big, beautiful home, a lassie dog...and no work. My sister, who was a Christian, said, "Where do you want to be?"

Outta my mouth, I blurted, "Calgary."

For some crazy reason, I had told my husband that we were being pulled to Calgary, and we would end up there. Little did I know, God was interested in getting us there and getting us saved in a hurry.

Now, you have to understand, there were not many jobs to be had anywhere. My sister asked which company my husband wanted to work for. I said, "Nova." She prayed.

Within a week or so, Nova contacted my husband. He had never even applied for a job with them. They said he didn't need to apply; they had a job for him. True story! Anyway, they set up a phone interview and basically hired him over the phone. The condition was that we had to relocate our family to Calgary.

The following day, I contacted a realtor. He came over and looked at our place. He said, "Rhéa, I'm gonna tell you something. You could be in this house for 10 months to three years because nothing is selling right now."

I called my sister and told her the news. She said, "God can sell your house in a day or in a week."

I remember I went up to my room and knelt by the bed and said, "God, my sister said You could sell our house in a day or in a week." I was going on someone else's faith, and God answered.

One week later, the realtor called. He said, "Rhéa, I have a buyer."

I said, "What? No one has even come to look at our place."

He said, "That's okay. This guy doesn't need to look at it. He just wants to buy it."

I thought to myself, *"That's crazy! Who would buy a house they have never even looked at?"* I thought that it was a ridiculous thing to do.

That night, the realtor came over. The fellow that wanted to buy our house was the previous owner. He and his wife had owned the place and went through a divorce. She got the acreage, and now he wanted it back.

We signed the papers. Our family and friends threw us a big farewell party. I cried a lot as I didn't really want to leave, but God was paving the way.

I never did get over the fact that fellow bought that place back without looking at it. I mean, we could have had wild parties (which we didn't) and had cigarette holes in the carpet (which we didn't). Funny thing is, he never knew why he bought that big place back. He put it on the market right away…and it took 10 months to sell it like the realtor had told us. All I could guess was that God had possessed him to buy it back so that we could get saved one month after moving to Calgary.

Yup, we got saved and filled with the Holy Ghost. (I guess if He is called a ghost, He could possess someone to buy their place back, right?)

We moved to Calgary in December 1990. You can imagine what a change that was, going from an acreage outside of a town of 5000-7000 people to a 1000 sq. ft. home in a large city. Big shock!

I had to learn to drive there on a three-lane freeway. My sister-in-law took me out one night, and I told her I was asking God to clear the freeway. She laughed. But you know, He cleared it about one mile in front of me and one mile behind me as I practiced learning the road that night. You eat an elephant one bite at a time, right? So, I conquered my fear of driving there.

I got saved in the wee hours of the morning on New Year's Day. My sister-in-law and brother-in-law invited us to a movie night at their church. I recall wearing a hot pink sweater and hot pink lipstick to match. In those days, I thought somehow that church people wanted you to be perfect. Although I'd been a good girl all my life, I thought they might pass out when they saw my lipstick. I said to my sister-in-law, "They will think I'm a harlot."

She said, "No, just come."

She was right. Crazy thing was...everyone was warm and friendly. I didn't really sense that they were pretending to like me. They even sat us on the front row.

The movie playing that night was called *China Cry*. It was about a woman who suffered persecution for her faith. It was good. I thought she was brave. After all, she survived a firing squad. That takes courage.

We went home, and my sister and brother-in-law brought some end-time videos. We watched one or two. At the end, there was an altar call. I remember saying to my sister-in-law, who I love, and my brother-in-law, "What if you are not ready?"

She said, "You will get left behind."

I was the type of person who never wanted to be left behind in anything. Remember, I was the 11th child of 12, so I already thought I was born late.

I told her I didn't want to be left behind. So, right then and there with them and the video hosts as my witness, I accepted Jesus Christ as my Lord and Saviour.

Immediately, it was like the lights went on. The following Sunday, I went forward during an altar call and made it public. A wonderful, kind woman recited the Lord's Prayer and reconfirmed to me that I was indeed saved and part of God's great big family and that all of Heaven was throwing a great big party to celebrate that. Well, I like parties, so I thought that was fun.

One week later, I went to a ladies' Bible study with my sister-in-law. At the end, they prayed, and I saw all these women move their lips in a quiet, mumbling way. Well, I was curious now.

On the way home, I asked my sister-in-law about it. She said they were praying in tongues. I asked if that was from God. She said, "Yes."

I said, "Then, I want it." So, the next Sunday at altar call time, I went forward. Yup, I got that "tongues" thing Johnny-on-the-spot.

I only got a few words, but my new friend said, "Keep saying it. You will get more."

She was right. By the end of that week, I had my new, full-blown heavenly language, and boy, did I use it! For me, it was like my world went from black-and-white TV to full-blown colour.

God immediately called me to Bible college. I found out I was pregnant with Baby #4 when I started Bible college. I knew God had called me, so I was determined to obey.

It was five days a week, Monday-Friday, 9:00 a.m. to noon. We had a kind lady—Miss Mary Annie—who looked after "Wee College" for our little ones. They loved her and learned a lot from her.

God had a plan—two attending for the price of one, me and my unborn child. He heard the Word of God preached in the womb for nine months. When he was born, my spiritual mom, Leita Ritch, wept for 20 minutes over him saying he was a "John the Baptist" and would warn many.

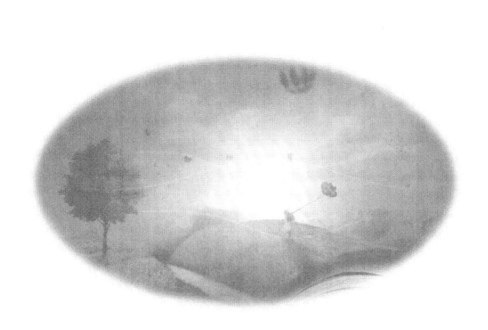

The Holy Ghost Speaks: "My Nephew" – Suicide

Shortly after getting saved, I got home from Bible college, and I heard the Holy Spirit say, "Arty[2] – suicide." I had a burden to pray in tongues. I prayed in tongues for three hours.

Three months later, my brother came to the city as it was the Calgary Stampede. My 12-year-old nephew was along. I said to him, "What were you doing on March—?" and I gave him the date and time. I said, "Were you suicidal?"

His 12-year-old eyes got huge. He said, "Auntie, you are not gonna believe this, but I had court that morning." (He got into trouble with the law for attention.)

He and my brother, his dad, were leaving the courthouse, and he said that he and his dad were fighting while flying down the highway at a great speed. My nephew suddenly opened the door and threw himself out. He then said, "Auntie, my dad didn't know what he would find when he came looking for me."

He got excited and big blue-eyed now. He said, "Auntie," and he did this hand thing across his chest (like when you are proud of someone). He continued, "My dad couldn't find a scratch on me." Arty said this in a very matter of fact and proud way with that big blue-eyed smile of his.

---

[2] Name changed to protect privacy

I said, "Boy, I *had* to pray for you." I led him to Jesus that week as he stayed with us. He and I had a lot of God talks over the years. I told him to call me collect from jail.

He did commit suicide several years later at 26 years old. He had a very hard life. I recall feeling helpless many times as I lived across the province from him. We did, however, go see him on many Sunday afternoons after church when he was in a young offender's prison. We could only do that when he was stationed in a facility near us.

I may never know why the Lord did not give me that same intercessory burden to pray so hard the night he hung himself in his apartment. Maybe Arty had had enough. I do know that my other nephew, Arlen[3], had reached out to him and bailed him out of jail. They would encourage each other in the Lord. Arlen got Arty to rededicate his life to Christ. Then he was gone.

I do believe in the mercy of God. God also knows when a human heart can't take anymore. I do believe God was there at that time.

Arty was like a spiritual son to me, one who could never get rid of his darkness. Due to the miles apart and not always knowing where or how he was, I had to trust God with his life.

When I got the phone call that he had committed suicide, I was angry. I remember having my head on the kitchen table and being angry. I was angry for a stolen life. I was angry for a stolen and lost destiny. I was angry for his stolen and lost seed—the children he should have had and those lost generations.

---

[3] Name changed to protect privacy

My spiritual daughter called at that time and played on her piano and sang the words "Your reward is in Heaven" for 45 minutes. That was a real comfort for me.

The next day, I painted a painting to explain his life at the open mike funeral. It was a non-Christian service, but I had to somehow let people know that the boy I knew had accepted Christ. I also wrote a poem/song for him to be read at his funeral. If I recall, it went like this.

What would I paint when I think of you?

What would I paint when I think of you?
Arty, what would I paint when I think of you?

Would I paint a stormy ocean?
Or would I paint the skies so blue?
(He had the bluest eyes.)
What would I paint when I think of you?

Would I paint a stained-glass window
With beauty in the air?
Or would I paint a shattered mirror
With pieces scattered everywhere?

I think I'd paint you sitting in Jesus' arms,
Totally safe and away from harm.
That's what I would paint when I think of you.

The painting was an acrylic 16x20. I painted a dark purple background, for he was royalty. I painted a bright sun on the top for the day he was born. In the center, I painted a cross for when he was 12 and accepted Jesus. I did paint red spots and cloudy, muddy colors overtop due to the fact that, whenever hope seemed to come, so did the darkness in his life to wipe it out and crush his hopes. At the bottom on the right, I painted several bottles of many shapes and explained at the funeral that Jesus promises to put all our tears in bottles[4] and that some folks will have more bottles of those tears in Heaven than others. Arty is one of those folks.

One day, I will get to see those brightest, bluest eyes again!

---

[4] See Psalms 56:8

"80-Year-Old Plumber"

Another child was born. As a growing family, we needed a larger house and yard for the children. Real estate had tripled in costs since we sold our acreage, so we rented a larger home with extra bedrooms. All was well for a short time.

Then, a leak sprung in the basement. The landlord called me back and said, "Rhéa, be up and ready by 8:30 a.m. cuz the plumber is coming over to repair the leak."

I said, "Okay."

The following morning, I was up and ready...but not nearly ready for what I was about to encounter. The doorbell rang, and I went to open it. To my surprise, when I opened the door, there on the front step was the cutest, elderly man. Seriously! It looked like he should have been in a senior's home or Extendicare. But there he was, a bit bent over with rolled up jeans and bright red, canvas sneakers. He held a lantern-type light with a cord.

What he said when he opened his mouth took me by surprise. He said, "PPPlumberrr."

As he stuttered, I stuttered back and said, "PPPardon me?"

I think we were both taken by surprise. Well, what does one do but let him in? I mean, seriously, he was harmless, and I was still in shock.

My 12-year-old son grabbed my shirt and said, "Mom, we better follow him." He had a worried look on his face as did I. I think we both knew that if we didn't follow him, somebody could get hurt, and it wouldn't be my son or me.

As I led him down the stairs, for we lived in a 4-level split, my mind was going wild. I thought, *"Oh no, if he falls off a ladder, he could die in my basement, and I could have blood everywhere, and I could get sued."* My almost adolescent son was having similar thoughts.

As we walked towards where the leak was, I pointed to the ladder. My son brought the ladder over. Really, it was more like a tall stool. This little, elderly gentleman plumber climbed it and stood on top. I thought, *"Lord, have mercy!"*

As I left the room, I told my son to watch him for a moment in case he fell. I returned to find him working on the leak, still standing on top of the stool with my son on standby as emergency help.

Shortly after this plumber entered the house, I recall thinking, *"Dear Jesus, this fellow is probably gonna die soon, and You want me to tell him about You so that he doesn't go to hell."*

I began to pace back and forth and back and forth, praying and asking God for boldness to tell him. As he walked up the stairs and passed the living room, I thought, *"This is it. I'm gonna tell him."* But...I chickened out.

It happened again as he was standing at the door...and then again on the front step. Each time I wanted to tell him, and each time I chickened out. After saying goodbye—and for the last time being a coward—I recall the sick feeling I had when I closed the door behind him.

I went to the kitchen and started repenting. I could see him dying and going to hell, and his blood would surely be on my hands. I had read that. Funny thing was, I was always witnessing to everyone back then, so I did not know why I couldn't tell him that day.

Suddenly, it was as though someone had turned the faucets on in my head, and I began to weep. I wept and wailed sitting on my kitchen floor. I wept and wailed a lot back then and told the boys that it was Mom praying. They would go play, but Gizmo, our chocolate miniature poodle, would always whimper for me at my side. Even my dog thought it was pitiful.

I told God that, if He would send him back, I would witness to him. I begged God to send him back. So, yup, you guessed it. It was probably a week later, that basement leak sprung again. This time when the landlord called, I was ready, armed, and dangerous. This plumber was gonna hear about my Jesus!

When he arrived, he said that he had to go back to his vehicle to get something. Again, I thought I should follow. The back of his truck was full of all kinds of spools. Well, put it this way, everything an 80-year-old could trip on and hurt himself good was in there. Plumbing supplies, I suppose. To this gal, it was a serious accident waiting to happen. The scariest thing was watching him walk through that maze. If you weren't praying before you saw a scene like this, trust me, you would be now. Calling all intercessors on the block or in the nearby vicinity, please!

So, he proceeded downstairs. This time, and for some reason, we had peace that he could handle it on his own. And he did.

As he came back up the stairs and headed out the door, I recall saying to myself, *"This time I'm gonna tell him, Lord."*

When I opened the door, his back was towards me as he went to take that first step. "Excuse me," I said. "Has anyone ever told you Jesus Christ loves you?"

There! It was out.

To my surprise, he said yes. I was surprised and said, "Oh, you know Him?"

And he said, "Yes, I do."

Then, for some crazy, odd reason, I decided to ask him in for tea. I would never have done this with a man in 1000 years but figured he was about 79 or 80 years old. He was too frail to harm me, and I had peace with it.

He came in and had tea with me and my kids. He proceeded to tell me of the miracles the Lord had done in his life. We had tea for an hour and a half that day. I sensed it was a very special time for us all. I felt honoured to have met him, to have him come back to my home and be able to sit with him.

Here I had wanted to tell him about Jesus, yet he was the one who taught me more about Jesus. He said he knew we were Christians because he had heard me say grace with my kids as he had walked by the kitchen.

I walked him out to his truck that day and made sure he got in okay since he had a high step to get up. He leaned out the window as he started the truck. Then, with a sobering tone that seemed to shift the whole atmosphere, he said, "Whatever you do, don't ever lose or give up your faith."

It sent chills up me. It was haunting, and I remember thinking as I have thought many times over the years... *"Lord, was that 80-year-old plumber an angel?"*

God's Sense of "Ha"

I worked as a children's minister for 14-15 years. Today, some of the kids I taught are lawyers, nurses, carpenters, writers, welders, policemen, etc. Never underestimate your ministry to teach, support, encourage, and love on the next generation. The fruit they produce will be fruit to your account.

The children were always excited and hungry. I loved working with the hungry, and children are fun. They have no pretense—they just say it like it is...right? I think Jesus likes that raw, sheer honesty.

Instead of celebrating Halloween, we always did a big Hallelujah night with fun, games, pizza, candy, etc. One year, my pastors came to me and asked if I could come up with an event. I quickly agreed despite not knowing what I would do. But with a big God who was very creative, surely something would come up.

Well, to my amazement, God inspired me to write a play. I got the download quite quickly. It was a comedy about how God's love changes you from the inside out. The 3 main characters were clowns. We had a clown in the play who was about to get saved. It was ridiculously funny.

I had had a prophecy once that, when I would speak, folks would at times fall outta their chairs laughing so hard. That happened at rehearsals as one of my clown accomplices fell out of her chair laughing so hard at the script and our bloopers.

The event night came. Many families came out with their children. We performed the play, and there was much fun and laughter had by all.

When the time came to do the altar call...well, there I was in my big old clown suit with a flashy, black-sequined blazer, huge duck feet slippers, and I was holding a rubber chicken and an annoying bike horn. I had a rainbow-colored wig on and larger-than-life, ruby red lips.

As I stood there and gave the altar call, friends of mine got saved. I mean adult friends, ones who I had tried for years to get saved. They wouldn't get saved by regular ol' me, but they got saved through me as a clown. I mean, can you believe that?

I thought kids would get saved, but adults got saved. I still find it amazing that I was somehow believable to them in that over-the-top, ridiculous outfit...but God knows best what bait to use to catch fish. Sometimes, I think He wants to tickle your funny bone and theirs too.

Another time, our home group decided to do an outreach for single moms in a poor neighbourhood in Calgary. Again, I put on my clown outfit—rainbow wig, duck feet, and all. I did all the usual silly stuff, songs, etc.

It was a sweltering hot day, and I needed a break. My pastor's wife and I decided to get away from the event and take a walk behind the scenes. We were standing by a fence chatting. Suddenly, a man on a bicycle came by. When he saw us, he stopped.

"What are you doing here?" he asked.

"We are telling people about Jesus," I said boldly as I slapped the fence.

"I want to know about Jesus," he said.

So, right then and there, my friend and I led him to Christ. Little did I recall what I was wearing, and my ruby red lips were probably ready to melt off my face. He didn't seem to mind at all, and looking back, the outrageous costume was probably the bait God used to have him stop and question us. I mean, how many times have you run into a clown on your bike path? God is so creative. I think we really need to think outside the box to catch some fish.

I grew up with a fishing family. We mostly did ice fishing in winter. Some fish like corn, some like cheese, and some like big, fat dew worms.

The harvest of souls is similar. Some will buy into it when we find out the bait they are waiting for. Maybe it's comedy, doing life together, etc. God will show us if we really desire to know.

Proverbs 11:30 says, *"The fruit of the righteous is a tree of life, and he who wins souls is wise."*

"I've got rivers of Living Water, and I've got a good-looking liver!"

November 1996

In the early fall of 1996, I noticed that I was unusually tired. I had to lay down for naps after lunch and then be in bed by 7:00 p.m. every night. Somehow, I knew something was wrong. You see, all my life I had been a hyper, go-go-go person with boundless energy—somewhat like Tigger on Winnie-the-Pooh. This was different.

After chatting with a friend, she recommended I go see her medical doctor/naturopath friend. I booked an appointment. To my surprise, she found out my liver was shot.

I asked her, "What next?"

She said, "Probably liver cancer."

I sat in that chair across from her and made up my mind. That was not the way it was gonna be. You see, I had read my Bible, and it taught me in Isaiah 53:5 that *"by His stripes we are healed."* And Psalms 103:3 says He *"heals all my diseases"* (NLT), and I knew I did not receive this report. That doctor could have proof (and she did), but I had a perfect outcome coming to me somehow.

Well, the funny thing is, I can tell you one thing I learnt from this experience. God is rushing your healing to you before you even know you need it. You see, about three weeks prior to that doctor's diagnosis, God had booked me into revival meetings (the Toronto Blessing) at Toronto Airport Christian Fellowship.

Three weeks prior to that doctor's appointment, my husband's company had a course they wanted him to take in Nashville, Tennessee. One day, he called me from his work, asking me if I would like to go to Nashville. I said, "No." It wasn't because I didn't want to go to Nashville. It was just that I didn't want to leave my boys for a week to 10 days. He said he would call his mother, the boys' grandma, and I should call my sister-in-law to see if they could each take two boys. They lived five minutes apart, and if they could see each other during the week, they wouldn't miss us so much. So, I agreed to call my sister-in-law. Well, they both agreed that each would take two boys. Plans were made, and to save the company $1000.00, it worked out to spend the weekend in Toronto.

We had a nice week in Nashville. I even got selected from a large crowd to do a TV commercial with Gary Chapman, host of Prime Time Country. That was a God thing for my kids and my momma's heart as you'll see in a minute.

Business folks on the trip told us we should go see the country band Alabama live on Prime Time Country. We got tickets and went for something to do. Well, before the show started, some of the crew members came out to excite the crowd and actually tell them when to cheer and when to clap. Well, I thought I could do that. They said the louder the better. I thought, *"Well, nobody here knows me, so yeah, I can do that too."*

Little did I know, they were scanning the live studio audience for the most excited audience fan. And to my surprise, they thought it was me. So, they came and told me I was selected to do a live commercial with the host of the show. He was a famous man.

I said, "No way!" They begged and pleaded, and everyone around me said go. So, I did.

Little did I know how God would use that commercial in the middle of the trip so that my boys could see their mom. We called home, and the boys got to see me that night on TV, so they didn't have to miss me.

Also, about six weeks later, it was Christmas. It was the first Christmas I couldn't see my parents. Boxing Day was their anniversary. My stepfather had fallen asleep in his armchair. Mom jumped up and said, "Henry, Henry! That's Rhéa!" Sure enough, it was a rerun of the show, and my parents saw me Christmas Day and so did their lonely friend halfway across the country as well as another elderly friend in another province. So, God used that commercial to comfort folks I cared about when I couldn't be there because He knew my heart was to be with them.

Leaving Nashville, we headed to the "Festival of Joy" in Toronto at the Toronto Airport church. The revival was full on and truly awesome. I got hit with laughter and laughed so hard during worship the first morning.

There were three ladies from Switzerland who walked to the meeting with us. We were all at the same hotel, so we decided to sit together.

During worship, a gal got slain in the Spirit not far from me, and it looked like she was hugging a pillar near her. That was a funny enough sight, but then she started yelling quite loudly, "He really, really, really, really loves me!" I mean, she did this repeatedly and very loudly. Well, that just cracked me up. It hit my funny bone that there was this gal who was wrapped around a pillar while lying on the floor who got hit with the Father's love. I loved it and joined in her joy. I laughed and laughed and laughed. I mean, I did so for about 20 minutes—unexplainable, sheer, heavenly, belly laughter. It was hilarious!

The worship ended, and people found their way back to their seats...if they could. If you've ever been in revival meetings, you would understand this. I don't think that gal made it back to her seat, but I did.

When I sat down, this middle-aged woman from Switzerland came and grabbed me. She said, "When I saw you laugh so hard, I said, 'Oh, Lord, I wish I could laugh like that.'" She said, "You see, I lost my husband three years ago."

Well, she cried, and I hugged her and cried and told her she would laugh again. Guess what? On the third day in the morning service, she got hit with the joy and laughed and laughed and laughed. Of course, I joined in there too. Oh, what fun to see my sister free! He who the Son sets free is free indeed!

On the Saturday night, they had a healing service. After worship, they said, "Anyone who needs healing in their bodies, stand up. Somebody will come and pray for you." So, I stood up. Two men came and laid hands on me and prayed for me.

Well, the power of God hit my body. It was like tremendous volts of electricity were going through my body, and I shook about 1000 miles an hour. They asked my husband if I had ever shaken like that before. He said, "No."

Well, I was healed. I mean, I was *totally* healed, and I *knew* it. I sang all the way home on the plane, "I've got rivers of Living Water," I told everyone, "and I've got a good-looking liver." And I did!

I knew when I got home and went to my checkup that my Christian doctor would almost fall outta her chair. She ran tests and yup, she almost fell outta her chair. I said, "It's a miracle, isn't it?"

She said, "It's a miracle." We rejoiced over what God had done.

So, you see I had not planned that trip. God had ordained it, but I had to participate and get to where the river was flowing, and faith was in the atmosphere.

We need to partner with God, and He will work everything out.

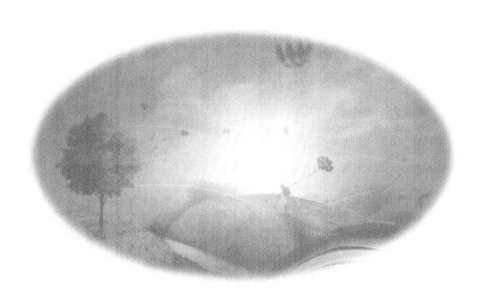

Joy for a Whole Year

Now looking back, I recall our church being in a renewal time also. Joy was being poured out in 1996. I, however, seemed to have an unusual amount of it. I laughed everywhere and all the time. God was doing a lot of healing and warfare with that laughter and joy. I mean, I laughed in hotels, elevators, parks, cars, and just everywhere. It was awesome!

Little did I know that God was preparing me for the next year of my life. Actually, all that supernatural joy was strengthening me for what I would go through in the next year of my life.

House Fire

March 20, 1997

When we got saved, we were radical givers. I understood a little what Ecclesiastes 2:26 in the Amplified version says. Yup, from what I understood, we were sinners who had been given the task to gather up some wealth and hand it over to the ones who please God. God began to teach us about investing into the Kingdom of God. Sowing and reaping is huge in the Kingdom.

I was raised on a farm, and us kids had to steward about a half-acre garden or more. So, I knew that you reap what you sow in there. Corn seeds grew corn stalks, and then you harvested ears of corn. Bean seeds grew beans, and pea seeds grew pea pods. Potato seeds made me the happiest though. I was eager to dig those potatoes, and as my stepfather used to say, "Rhéa, if all we fed you was potatoes, you would be very happy."

I used to say, "Yes." I could have lived on potatoes. I could have probably produced a potato cookbook if I had wanted to…I mean, baked potatoes, mashed potatoes with dill & cream, potato wedges, potato skins, French-fried potatoes, and the list goes on. You see, I saw those cut up potatoes we put in the ground as a potato Jubilee every time. It seemed like we had a bumper crop each year.

So, when I learned these "giving" principles, it was like common sense went out the door. I had always been a giver, but there was no stopping me now. We even gave away the down payment for a house.

Our pastor came up to me one day and said, "You guys should think about buying a house." I mean, he knew we were just about giving away the farm so to speak.

I said, "Pastor, who needs a house?"

Jesus is coming soon. Well, the good news is that our God keeps good accounts. Heaven is into numbers. God created a whole book on His giving love in the most amazing ways. We as His kids ought to be the most generous folks in the world if we truly want to imitate Him.

Now, the devil started to come around shortly after some ridiculous giving. He would say things like, "Who do you think you are doing that? You will never have a house now. Look at you...you will be poor, and your kids won't have a roof over their heads."

You have to press through that and say, "Shut up, devil! My God will bless me as He has promised. Get outta my way! I'm pressing through, busting through, and breaking through."

We prayed, kept giving, and held onto the promises of God to give us a home. We also began saving for another down payment. Several years went by when suddenly a door opened. We had been praying as to where to live in the city and felt God was calling us to a certain area. We found a builder, found a lot, and began the process of building a house.

We moved into our new home on December 20, 1996. Exactly three months later, on March 20, 1997, we awoke to our house totally on fire. It was the loudest thing I have ever experienced.

When three sides of your house and the roof of your house are on fire? Trust me! It's louder than a jet plane taking off (if you are sitting in the back row). I mean, it's outrageously loud!

We literally woke up, and three sides of the house and the whole roof was on fire. In another five minutes, I would have had to jump for my life out of a second story window, and we would have lost all our children. We had one door left to get out. When we ran outta that door, the flames were coming at us.

A few friends of ours felt troubled for two months to three weeks before the fire. They kept asking us if our family was okay. I replied, "Yes, we are fine." They said they really had to pray for us. Looking back, I knew their intercession had saved our lives.

The story of our house fire hit the news, which in some ways added more trauma as I was a shy and private person. Reporters came to the friends who had taken us in. I recall them asking how I could still be smiling that day as my family had just lost everything in the earthly world. My reply was simple: "Yes, we lost everything here on this earth, but that fire couldn't take Jesus from me."

I think the hardest thing as a mom was knowing my children had lost 100% of everything they loved and owned. They were four to twelve years old and had lost every teddy bear, blankie, Tonka truck, etc. I remember after the fire, one of my boys put his bunny down on a stair one night after being tucked in. I asked him why he put his new bunny on the stairs. He said, "In case there is another fire, I can quickly grab him." I cried.

How you really feel about life is what will come outta your mouth when you go through life's fires on this earth. We are living in a day and hour when everything that can be shaken is being shaken.

I was on a trip home recently where I heard stories of people losing their jobs left, right, and centre. It is helpful through those storms when we, who have known loss, can comfort and encourage them, stand with them, and pray for them.

I have moved over 40 times in my life. That is a lot of loss of homes, friends, and communities. But do you know what? I have friends in many places. I also have had the opportunity to decorate a lot of homes, which enabled me to help others decorate their homes. It's all about perspective. Yes, I have known much loss, but by God's grace, I have experienced recovery. I can say, "He has given me beauty for ashes, joy for mourning."

God Knows when
You Are in the Dump

After the house fire, I slowly learned to receive. This is very humbling when you love to give, right? Now, my entire family was on the receiving end of folk's benevolence.

About two years after the fire, God called us to move to a different town. It was a bit of a hidden place, and folks in the city barely knew this place existed 45 minutes away.

While there, we joined a church who prayed for our family. They had friends in Romania who wanted to build an orphanage. Having spoken about children at risk for years and having researched many nations on the subject, I was all in. I told the pastor's wife we should have a church garage sale to raise money for them. She said, "Okay, but you organize it," which I did.

As I went through some of our family's things to contribute, I sensed the Lord nudge me to let go of my funeral clothes. I instantly knew what He meant. You see, when you go through a huge trauma such as a house fire and losing every earthly possession, you are grieving. People give you their clothes, and while it's nice for a while, you are grieving. And trust me, science has proven matter has memory. So, guess what? The clothes I had inherited were now mostly grieving.

While they wouldn't harm others, they somehow kept reminding me of my loss. We didn't have a lot of extra money then. So, I knew that as I let go of each item in my closet, the Lord Himself would have to get me a new wardrobe. And He did!

Our pastor had always said to listen to your children as God can speak through them. One day, my son came home from school and said very insistently, "Mom, we gotta go to the dump *now*."

I didn't question but figured he knew something I didn't. You see, I worked part-time in a craft antique store then. My son had seen an old man from town rummaging in the dump and knew he came to my store to consign his goods, and he did well on that. My boy decided to do that also. I thought he felt he would find something right then and there.

So, off we went—just him and I. After looking around to no avail, he decided to look in the "take it or leave it" recycle shed. There, lying on the floor, were three black garbage bags. He said, "What's in there?"

We proceeded to look, and to my amazement, there were some of the most beautiful clothes I had ever seen. Some had brand new tags, like a navy, thick-laced dress did. There was a Joseph coat of many colors and clothes all in my size. There in the dump that day sat my new heavenly wardrobe.

I still recall when a lady who was high up on a ladder in a high-end mall saw me wear that coat of many colors and yelled, "Hey, where did you get that coat?" She almost fell off her ladder. I thought, *"Lady, if you only knew."*

So, what's holding you back? Are you still hanging onto faded memories and your funeral clothes, or are you going to let go of the old and let God bring in the new?

For all I know, angels could have flown my new wardrobe in, but I had to make a choice to let go of the old first.

Shopping for His Heart

There are numerous things to replace after the loss of a house and every earthly possession for six people after a house fire. While you can live without much here in Canada, many of us have insurance which does help replace most things. It did take a while to rebuild, refurnish, and replace a home, clothes, toys, dishes, bikes, etc. We all got shopped out—yes, including me. I didn't care to see any more stores.

One day, I had my youngest son with me who was about five at the time. I told him we had to go to the mall so that I could get something I needed. Well, as it is with many of us women, we get our item, but then we stop at two, three, or four more stores. This time, I stopped at several stores before I got to the store where I had originally needed to go.

As I was leaving the store, my son, who had been so patient, quiet, and good about my errands, piped up. He said quietly, "Well, Mommy, with a whole lot of stalling and a little bit of shopping, we finally got it done."

That was an "aha" moment for me because I have thought about it a lot over the years. It was very clever and smart of my son to have figured out and observed that and then quietly bring it to my attention.

I have recently thought, *"Lord, is that how we are or act when seeking or shopping for what's on Your heart—the item or items for that day? Do we start out with good intentions, only to get derailed, sidetracked, and busy before finally getting to what is really important? Really, what we set out to shop for early in our devotional time is the agenda on Your heart...but how much are we focused on that? Like I did that day, do we get bombarded by everything else that looks good and needs our attention and actually forget why we came?"*

Matthew 6:33 says, *"But seek first the kingdom of God and His righteousness, and all these things shall be added to you."*

A Lesson Learned from the Fire

After the fire, we stayed with our pastors for three weeks. I was humbled as women brought clothes and casseroles to their house. I recall crying one day a few weeks later when I realized I didn't have a kitchen much less a stove to cook anything for anyone. I was humbled to be on the receiving end.

My pastor called me aside then. He said, "Rhéa, have you been healed of rejection?"

I said, "Yes, I have, but this receiving Is hard and humbling." You see, I loved to give all the time, but now I had nothing to give.

He said, "If you love to give, then you have to learn to receive." That was a lesson I learned and am still learning.

We stayed in our friends' home for three weeks while they went on vacation. We then rented a home while we rebuilt another house on the same spot as the fire. We could have gone anywhere in the city, but we felt that was where God wanted us, so we went back. While it had been an extremely cold winter, and we really didn't know anyone there at all, we just felt we were to be there. Then, neighbours we didn't know set up a trust fund.

Meanwhile, at the rental home, my son started selling candy out of our garage. He set up a daily candy store and would open the garage for an hour or two. The children from the neighbourhood would line up. It was a God idea. They would get some sweets, and I would share Jesus with them.

One day, there was a knock at the door. It was a neighbour I had never met before. She said she lived two houses away from where ours had burnt. She felt so bad and guilty as they were trying to get their TV and stuff out of their garage while our house was fully inflamed. She had watched as we came out from the back of the house (our last door to get out from), and the flames were coming out at us then. She had brought some food, toiletries, and toys for our boys. I told her it wasn't her fault, and we were okay as we were rebuilding our second house in 15 months and trying to rebuild our lives.

We went to the framed new house one day. It was on location of the fire. A bunch of neighbours we had not met (who lived there during the fire) had gathered. They saw us pull up to the construction site. They were quiet as we got outta our car. Again, we had not met them due to an extremely cold winter when people just leave their houses to go to work then drive into their garage, eat, sleep, and stay inside.

Suddenly, a few of them came over to us—very sad—and introduced themselves to us. They said they were very sorry for our house fire and felt really bad since they had watched our house burn.

I remember trying to not let my eyes get too big. I silently said, *"God, don't let my eyes get big."* I recall being horrified as I heard how they had had to live with their guilt. I was shocked. Totally!

I mean, I thought, *"We could have almost died and lost all of our children, and they all watched our house burn and didn't tell us."*

They didn't yell, try to throw a rock in a window, or climb in to save us. I thought of what I imagined I would do if I saw someone's house on fire. I mean, I would jump, yell, and try to get help. But she said they just stood there watching.

We spoke a bit, and then we went into the stick-framed, drywalled house. I thought, *"I have to forgive them."*

Instantly, the Lord spoke to me something very haunting. He said, "Rhéa, if you and your family would have died in that fire, you would all be with Me, right?"

I said, "Yes, Lord."

He then replied, quite calmly but seriously, "If you don't tell them about Me, they themselves are 'their house,' and you are watching their house burn, and they will go to hell, right?"

I said, "Yes, Lord, enough said." I got that big time! By the time we left that cul-de-sac, seven of the ten households were saved or walking again with the Lord.

We need to tell our neighbours about Christ. If we don't, we are watching their houses burn, and they themselves are their own walking, physical houses. Wow! That's powerful and convicting. There is eternity to fill and hell to plunder for our Lord.

Are you watching people's houses burn? I know at times that I am. We will be held accountable.

It's easy to give away the free gift that we have been given. All it takes is for us to open our mouths. In Luke 9:26, Jesus says, *"whoever is ashamed of Me",* He will be ashamed of when He comes. If we don't tell them about Jesus, and they go to a Christless eternity, then we ourselves are watching their houses burn. It's scary and thought-provoking but true. So, let's plunder hell and watch them burn for our Lord.

Face-to-Face Encounter

Most of my life as a believer has been spent in intercession. I was saved in a praying church, and the spirit of prayer took over my life. My earlier walk included morning devotions from 4-7:00 a.m. before I woke up my children to homeschool. The church we attended had early morning prayer from 6-8:00 a.m. a few mornings a week.

If you dedicate your life to Him, He will meet with you. If He sees you are serious about your time with Him and are faithful, well, you will see miracles, signs, and wonders and know Him like never before.

After meeting with the Lord faithfully for years and after experiencing several encounters and life-changing ways of God, He came to me face to face.

One evening as I was lying in bed, the Lord came instantly into my room. It was the Lion, fierceness and all. My body began to shake about 1000 miles an hour. The entire time, I felt a sense of wonder and terror. I recall it feeling way more terrible than wonderful. I thought I would die the whole time. I literally did not know how or when I would catch my next breath. I was shaking so hard that I could not utter a single word. I didn't know when it would end.

The Lord got into my face and spoke very sternly. It was intentional, and He was about to reveal more of my destiny and calling. And I needed to obey Him whether I liked it or not. He was a Lion…and I was a woman who was about to gain an understanding of His fierceness and His mandate for my life. I remember feeling so small and delicate in His awesomeness of power.

As He came closer and right in my face, He said:

1. *You will be a spokesman to the Nations.*

2. *You will warn many.* (This was not optional; neither was the 1st one.)

3. *From now on, you will tremble.*

With this last sentence, He was clearly and seriously letting me know that what He did to my body when He touched it in the future was none of my business. It was not for me to control it, nor would I be able to. He was clearly God and would also be Lord of my body.

I have never ever been the same since that day. You see, you cannot be touched by thousands of volts of heavenly electricity and ever be the same. It simply cannot be.

Healed of Insomnia

A few years after that encounter, we moved. We began to do renovations on this home that was begging to be updated.

Almost overnight, it seemed as though I developed insomnia. My intercession seemed to grow from a few hours a day to 6-10 or 12 hours per day. I only slept about two hours per night. I am not sure how I managed except by the grace of God. This went on for a few years.

One night—well, actually in the wee hours of the morning at 4:00 a.m.—I awoke. I could see and feel this bright light coming from the front door and right up the stairs, right to where I lay in bed. To my surprise, I could also hear many voices singing, and I had a knowing that there were many angels (between 10 to 100) on my front doorstep. The exact amount I do not know, but there were many. They were singing three words that started with the letter H—one was 'Hallelujah', one was 'Hosanna', and one was 'Holy'. They sang these words over and over and over again.

I fell asleep and woke up at 9:00 a.m. I got up and couldn't help but sing what they had sung on my doorstep. I sang from 9:00 a.m. 'til noon that day...and then slept like a baby from that day onward. I was totally and instantly healed of insomnia and have been totally healed ever since.

Psalms 103 talks about His ways being higher than our ways. I do not know why God sent all those angels to sing on my doorstep, but they gave me the words to sing for my own healing. I'm not sure if it was their singing combined with mine that brought the breakthrough but, "Thank You, Lord, I'm healed! Thank you, Jesus!"

A United Effort

God gave me a verse when I lived in Airdrie from the book of Jeremiah. It said to pray for the peace and prosperity of the city to which He had called me to. I took that seriously.

I started a prayer group for Canada in my home, and now intercessors from the city began to have a desire to pray together for our city. We did gather to meet, and we also did a bit of research. We found out that the first Church in Airdrie was the United Church. It was united indeed. You see, history books told us that it was built on First Avenue and First Street, and it is still there today. Several congregations from different denominations got together to build that little church. Then, each denomination used it a different night of the week. Apparently, revival did break out there for a bit.

Could it be that way back then, God liked what He saw—brothers dwelling together in unity—and He decided He would come down and kiss that place with His presence? They had something many places are trying to achieve now. Young people started to come to those city-wide prayer meetings.

81

Totem Poles and the Inuit

July 2007

One day, I picked up a newspaper, and to my surprise, the mayor had agreed to have totem poles made and shipped from overseas. I just knew we needed to pray about this.

Our particular city was stated online to be the highest elevated city in our province, but some thought maybe in our whole nation.

The intercessors from the city gathered around the totem poles in the park to pray. Suddenly, I fell to my knees and cried out to God saying, "God, the Inuit have to come." Somehow, my spirit knew we needed them, and the weight of the glory they carry as gate keepers to our nation for this.

A few days later, a friend called and said, "Rhéa, I've got two van loads of Inuit with me. Where do you want me to bring them?"

I called the intercessors, and they were in awe saying, "Rhéa, remember you cried out to God to send them a few days ago?" They reminded me that I had fallen to my knees, and my spirit had cried out to God loudly to send them.

Heaven responded before that prayer, for it says in the Bible in Isaiah 65:24 that He answers before we ask.

Gold Dust

I knew something was up with the Lord. You see, for quite a while, I had been having gold dust appear on my hands and upper arms. At times, even larger flakes appeared on my face.

In this season, I remember going into the city one day singing a silly love song I had made up for the Lord. I sang it all the way as I drove. When I returned home, to my amazement and surprise, my kitchen floor was covered in gold dust. Immediately, I ran downstairs to ask my two younger children who were in high school if they had been playing with glitter. They replied, "Mom, we haven't had glitter in the house since we were kids."

I ran back upstairs and grabbed a large black cloth and began to wipe the floor. It was amazing! I put some of it into a container.

During this same time, lightning bolts would come through my windows. At night while I was sleeping, it was like my spirit knew when they were coming. I would wake up, and I would half sit up in my bed about a split second before they would appear. Again, Heaven was invading the piece of earth where I dwelt.

Another evening, I was awoken to huge fireballs outside my bedroom window. It was like they would come down and dance. I did not realize 'til years later that Psalms 18:12-14 in the Message translation speaks of fireballs and that *"He hurls lightnings"* down. It is also referred to in numerous other places in the

Word, like in Revelations Chapter 8. It would not be 'til many years later that the Lord would reveal to me why this was happening at this time in my life.

Back to the Inuit

As a child, we learned about the Inuit in school. Then as a youth, I had a young Inuit friend who was deaf. I could only see her every two weeks, but we laughed a lot together as she tried to teach me sign language. Years later, I was given an Inuit skating ornament for my Christmas tree. God had a plan and had given me a love for them, and now I was about to meet them.

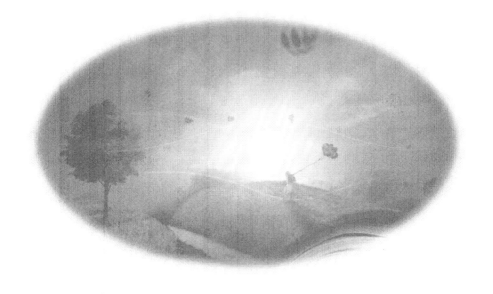

Lightning Bolts and Fireballs

During the same time when the gold dust appeared and covered my kitchen floor, it had also been showing up daily on my hands and sometimes even up my arms. Once, I had 3 larger flakes appear on my face.

This was a special time with the Lord as I had that really bad insomnia for those years and just felt humbled every time God showed me His glory in that way. Sometimes, I have wept as I didn't know why God did that, but I think He just wanted to remind me He was with me. It always humbles me when He does this.

The week prior to the Inuit coming, I also had lightning bolts come through my house and fireballs (massive ones) appear outside my bedroom patio doors. It was a wild, wonderful, mysterious time with God. He just kept surprising me.

When the lightning bolts came into my bedroom (and by the way, you will find this in Psalms 18:14), I always knew a split second before they would come as I would awaken then. It was like my spirit man knew when Heaven was sending them, and every time I would wake up a split second before they would come into my room and appear right over me.

One time, there were three large ones right in a row. Another time, as I was visiting with someone in my kitchen, one appeared.

I didn't know why this was happening but found out years later that God was indeed taking me outta an ocean of hate like He says in His Word. I was being separated and cut away beginning at that time. It brought about major shifts in my life.

The last lightning bolt came when I was on crutches and had to sleep in the home of a woman who had been very abusive to me. I had to sleep on her couch as I couldn't sleep in a regular bed due to my leg injury. That night, a large lightning bolt came right over me in that house. I woke up a split second before. I didn't realize 'til years later what that would all mean, but I thank my God that He knew what He was up to. He was about to set me free.

These events also had to do with the Inuit that God was bringing into my life. They brought love, life, freedom, and joy.

We got a room at a Catholic church and hosted a reconciliation and repentance meeting for what we as Canadians had done to the Inuit, our own people.

They—like my ancestors, the Acadians—had had their families ripped apart and children stolen from them. The Inuit were driven from their land to live in inhuman conditions and places where it was 70 below, they had no sled dogs (for they had been shot), and they had only tents and no way to access food. Some of those folks died of broken hearts. It is no small miracle that any of them survived, and God and only God could have done that.

As we asked for forgiveness and repented, many were healed, and we wept and held each other. There was healing for all. Thank you, Lord!

I hosted several of them in my home. The next morning when I went to make brunch, the eggs in my fridge were all solidly frozen. I went to get another dozen, and they also were as solid as ice. We all laughed as I showed them this when I went to crack the eggs to make an omelette. I had never had that happen before nor has it happened since.

I found it interesting that they came from the land of snow and ice, and here my eggs were frozen. God knew we used ice for comfort, right? He knew "egg-actly" what we needed!

Their apostolic leader had us pray and told me he wanted me to come to the Arctic to ordain me. They are "Gate Keepers" in that land. He said he knew who I was and that was what God had shown him. He also knew that my people's voice had not been heard in Canada for 400 years. He had heard of the Acadians, which I was.

I wept that morning at the table as I had done some research, and God had just shown me this about myself and my people. This man of God knew and recognized me by the Spirit of God.

This is what is missing today in the Body of Christ. We must look past the outer man and recognize who people are in the spirit realm. They are not the earth suit they are walking around in.

There is a rank and file in any army. In the heavenly realm, it is no different. Some people you treat like privates are actually five-star generals, and some whom you worship as five-star generals are privates who have learned to act and use all the lingo. We must learn to tell the difference. This will make all the difference in how effective an army we will be for the Kingdom of our God.

It's time we line up rank and file behind our King and effectively impact the earth and populate Heaven.

Commanding Tornadoes to Cease

I was on a trip to the U.S.A. en route to hear Kenneth Hagin. I was with a friend, and we flew to Dallas and then drove to Jackson, Mississippi. On the way back, we ended up in Houston.

We were in the hotel one day when the Holy Spirit said we had to get outta that hotel "right now!" We packed up promptly and got outta there.

A short time later, there were flash floods in the area. From the new place where we were situated, we watched the news and saw that 22 counties were under water. The hotel we had been at was one of the flooded places. Thank you, Lord, because when those flash floods come down there in Texas, we found out people could drown in their cars. It happened to a pastor's daughter while we were down there. I am thankful I heard God's voice and obeyed.

Another wild deliverance of the Lord happened while down there when we went to spend a night on Galveston Island. We witnessed to some kids on the beach the first night. The next morning, we got up and went for a walk on the beach again. We got back to our hotel, and there was a loud, eerie siren sound coming out of the TV. Now, I had never heard of that coming out of a TV in Canada my whole life. So, this caught my attention!

We heard on TV that a hurricane was coming to Galveston Island, and we had to evacuate the island. Again, we packed up but somehow had peace. The Holy Spirit said, "You've got time to stop for lunch." So, we grabbed a bite and headed off the island.

Suddenly as we were driving, two funnel clouds appeared on each side of the car. A righteous anger rose up within me, and I pointed my finger and said, "In the name of Jesus, you cease your manifestation." Immediately, a horizontal line came right across the bottom of those tornadoes like a line was being drawn in the sand to cut those things off.

We have got to wield our swords in this hour and use the miracle in our mouths and the name of Jesus. You had better believe it! It works!

Storms will come our way, but if you know who you are and whose you are, you can make these things bow down in Jesus' name. This world is counting on the sons and daughters of the living God and so is our God!

By taking your authority over storms, you may be able to save people from going to a Christ-less eternity. They may be granted prolonged lives and so might you. They may gain other chances to hear the Gospel and want to hear about your miracle-working God.

Jesus at Tim Horton's

A few years back on a hot summer day, I drove outta town to meet a friend for coffee. We chose to meet at Tim Horton's. I arrived early and parked my jeep. As soon as I had parked, I noticed a man come walking over to the side where I had parked. He appeared suddenly out from the back corner of the building. As he came around the building, our eyes locked. He looked like a homeless man, although he was fairly tidy with a backpack on. He had dreadlocks and the most piercing blue eyes I have ever seen.

I thought, *"Surely You want me to tell him about You tonight, Lord."* Or so I thought.

I proceeded to go in, get some tea, and sit down in a far corner. It was a really large Tim Horton's. Although it was the supper hour, the place was empty.

Suddenly, I saw the door open, and there was the homeless man. He went to the counter and ordered a drink. I didn't think much of it and went on daydreaming.

As he walked over towards my table, I noticed he had a drink and a very large box. He asked if I would mind if he sat at the table right beside me. I said, "Sure, go right ahead."

He sat down, opened the large box, and inside was one dozen of the most celebratory, colourful donuts you could ever have picked. Now, it was the supper hour, and I would have thought he might have bought soup or chili or something, not 12 large, party-style donuts. Interesting.

He proceeded to start eating one of those donuts and grabbed a nearby newspaper. He quietly laughed and really seemed to be enjoying the donuts and the comic section of the paper. I was thinking, *"Surely, Lord, You want me to tell this guy about You tonight? I mean, this big place is totally empty except for me and him, right? And he is having dessert for dinner."* It was all kind of starting to feel like it does when God sets you up with divine appointments.

"Who is gonna start the conversation?" was my next question. *"Well, it might as well be me, so here goes,"* I thought.

"Are you new here?" I asked.

"Yes," he replied. "Just got into town now."

"Funny," I thought, *"so did I."*

"You looking for work?" I asked.

"Oh no," he said, "I'm much too busy for that. Want a donut?" he asked as he turned his box to offer me one.

"That's okay," I said, "I don't eat wheat."

He continued to chuckle softly to himself while reading the comic section and eating his donuts. It was interesting and amusing to watch. He really did seem quite content with himself and with life.

"This is it," I thought, *"Here goes again."*

"Has anyone ever told you about Jesus?" I asked.

"Um hum," he replied nodding.

"So, you know Him?" I asked, surprised.

"Um hum," came the answer as he continued to read his paper and nodding his head up and down.

"So, did you grow up in the church?" I inquired.

"No," he said.

I then asked, "Well, do you go to any church?"

To which he replied, "Not many, I'm much too busy for that." He answered kindly but seriously.

Then outta the blue, he asks, "So, you going through a divorce?"

I almost jumped outta my skin but kept myself calm on the outside so that I wouldn't spill my tea. How did he know that? So, I asked him, "How did you know?"

He kept munchin' the donuts and reading the paper and said, "I figured."

This was getting kind of haunting—eerie but peaceful at the same time. I mean, here was this dreadlock-wearing man with the bluest eyes in the world who knew Jesus and was much too busy to work, much too busy to go to church, and knew exactly what I was going through. Wow!

I told him that whatever he had need of before we left, my friend and I would pray for him. (My friend was about 45 minutes late.)

Oh, and by the way, when I had asked the homeless man what his name was, he said, "Christopher." I knew that Christopher meant 'gift of God'.

When my friend arrived, Christopher asked if he should still sit there, and I said, "Sure."

I noticed throughout our visit that he continued to eat donuts and chuckle in amusement as he read the paper.

After about an hour and a half having tea with my friend, Christopher got up to leave. I said, "Hey, Christopher, we would like to pray for you. Is there anything you would like prayer for?"

He stood quietly and pondered for what seemed like quite a while. Then, he lifted his head and looked at me. "Is there anything I would like prayer for?" he repeated. He paused and repeated my question to himself.

He then said, "Would you please pray for my enemies?"

I nearly jumped again. In fact, I think I almost stuttered and said, "Pray for your enemies? Oh, Christopher, you are much nicer than I am!"

He just said quietly but very solidly, "Please pray for my enemies." With that, he walked out the side door.

Well, I was riveted on the inside. What had just happened? I don't think an angel would ask this, yet somehow, from then 'til today, I am still convinced that I met with Jesus at Tim Horton's.

He circled that coffee shop all the while I chatted with my friend. Before I left, I looked up and there was a huge, white, plume feather—like a writer's pen with a huge white feather—in the sky over top of where I stood.

The Kingdom of Heaven does have those that do not love it...yet. But Jesus' heart is so big that He wants us to pray for them.

It's also fun to know that He likes our Canadian Tim Horton's and its celebratory donuts.

Lost in a McDonald's Parking Lot (Seriously!)

In summer of 2015, I was on my way to Calgary to see my family. When I got to a certain town along the way, the Lord said, "Stop at McDonald's."

I said, "Lord, I'm not hungry," but I did know I could use the bathroom.

I walked into the bathroom, used the facility, and came out to wash my hands. I saw a distraught young gal who had just set a pregnancy test kit on the counter. She appeared very concerned.

I thought, *"Oh, oh! I know why I'm here now."*

I had to reach around her to grab a paper towel to dry my hands. I prayed for wisdom.

"Are you pregnant?" suddenly burst out of my mouth.

She nodded yes and got teary eyed. To my utter amazement, such excitement came over me, and I shouted, "Congratulations! That's so exciting!" Then, I hugged her.

Yup! Now I was hugging a total stranger and telling her that it happened to me, too, at 19 and how she would see God provide.

I asked if she had a husband, and she said, "No, just a boyfriend," one that she had just met.

Again, I said, "That's so exciting! God will provide."

I asked her if she liked the boyfriend, and she said yes. I said, "That's great! God will provide."

Well, we hugged and laughed and cried and hugged and laughed again. So, I figured my job was done with my new divine appointment.

I proceeded to leave and had to drive by the two newly expecting lovebirds. I rolled down my window and gave them a thumbs up and shouted, "That's great! God will provide." They hugged each other and laughed.

I went to leave the parking lot and literally couldn't see the exit, so I had to go around them again. So again, I rolled down the window, gave them thumbs up and gave my congratulations, pointed to Heaven, and reassured them that God was going to provide. They laughed and so did I.

Well, the third attempt to find the exit proved to be identical to the last two, even though this time they might have thought, *"Seriously, lady?"* We laughed our heads off as I did all the same thumbs up, words, and actions.

This was honestly like a scene from a Carol Burnett show. Truthfully, I literally couldn't find the exit! But somehow, I think God may have momentarily blocked me from seeing it to save the life of a child. His ways are higher than our ways. And one thing was for sure, the three of us had more than a few belly laughs that day.

300 Prodigals Come Home

I was invited by a prominent businessman to come and teach his prayer group about intercession. I was told to bring some of my paintings and that I could bring a friend if I wanted to. I asked a girlfriend who was also a prophetic artist to join me.

So, off we went for a car ride 1 ½ hours away. We prayed in tongues all the way there. Upon our arrival at this businessman's car dealership, we were greeted and ushered upstairs to the upper room he reserved for prayer.

We had some worship first. Then, my friend and I pulled out our art to share with them. My friend took out a painting she had done of prodigals with very heavy, sorrowful faces and pieces of broken glass along the bottom. She set it on the floor.

Well, a new pastor from town was there. He had moved to that town which was surrounded by about 120 covens. The oppression in the air was thick, and trust me, even with five cups of coffee a day in that area, you could hardly wake up.

When he saw that painting, he hit the floor so fast and began wailing. Then, several other men and a few women hit the floor, wailing and crying their guts out for prodigals to come home. That was on a Friday night.

There was also a woman there who looked like the deadest living woman I had ever seen. She stared into outer space, and I thought, *"Lord God, give her hope."* My girlfriend's daughter felt that we were supposed to gather around her chair and do a "freedom dance." So, we did. We played a song on a CD that cried out "Freedom!" and danced around and around her chair.

Well, when all was said and done, we got up and drove the 1 ½ hours home. The testimonies of what God had done rolled in shortly thereafter.

A few days later on the Sunday morning, that wailing pastor who had hit the deck went to his little church. He was in his study and studying and praying from 6-10:00 a.m. To his amazement, when he opened the door to go and preach, there were 300 prodigals in his church. He normally had about 6 folks in church. God had heard his cries. This new man in a new town with God's heart for the broken had broken through. Heaven heard. Yes, he had gotten their attention, and I believe God sent angels to gather in his harvest.

What do you cry out for? Don't stop! Heaven hears.

A few months later, I was at a conference. A beautifully dressed woman ran up to me and said, "Rhéa!" She threw her arms around me and cried and cried in my arms. She kept saying, "I'm free! I'm free!"

I did not recognize her and wondered who she was and how she knew me and my name. Then she said, "It's me," and she told me her name. Well, I just about fell over. I mean, here stood that woman from that meeting, the one who had looked dead to the world. She said that she had been in a six-year depression, and that night, she got delivered and set free. Praise God! She also looked about 20 years younger.

See, you do not know when God will call you or how He will use your little loaves and fishes to bless others. Your talents are meant to be shared, whether it's through broken imagery called art or a funny little made-up dance on the spot. Just do it...and watch Heaven invade earth.

"God says go! God says go!"

At Rosh Hashanah two years ago, I had a few dreams. One of the dreams had huge black letters in the sky that read "Liberty". I thought that was good because I was needing some of that.

The following year came, and in the summer, a friend of mine called and asked me to go to a conference in the U.S.A. I flat out said, "No."

She begged and pleaded for me to go, but I simply had no desire. She became insistent and said, "Did you pray about it?" and hung up.

I thought, *"Well, no, I didn't cuz I am fairly certain even God Himself doesn't want me to go to this one."*

Somehow that night, I felt a bit convicted about not asking the Lord about it. I knelt by my bed and prayed a simple one-liner like, "God, do You want me to go?"

In the wee hours of the morning, I woke up to about 10-12 large angels in my room yelling at the top of their lungs repeatedly, "God says go! God says go!" over and over. It was so loud that it startled me, and I immediately jumped out of bed and began to pack.

The Agenda
Behind the Agenda

In case you didn't know it, God often has one of these—an agenda behind the agenda. Little did I know that, exactly to the date 1 year after my dream, I would be going over the border and be in the U.S.A., the "Land of Liberty."

A few minutes over the border, my girlfriend said to stop the car. She had a funny feeling that we needed to run across the road towards some mailboxes. I didn't know why, but I trusted her.

When I looked down on the ground when we crossed, I saw a coin. I picked it up, and it said "Liberty" on it.

The conference was good. I laughed sooooo much for that whole week that I knew God was healing my heart even through laughter.

When you are on the frontlines of battle, your body goes there too. Laughter releases so much, and as the Bible says, it is like medicine[5]. So, God just poured and poured His medicine in me through laughing with a friend.

---

[5] See Proverbs 17:22

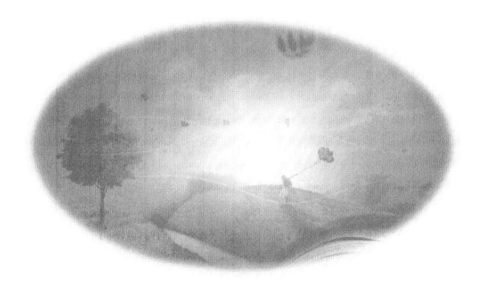

Bridal Shop Encounters

For a season of life after my kids had grown up, I worked as a bridal consultant. In fact, the morning my mother died was my first day of work at that place.

I got a call at 6:00 a.m. that February morning from my family saying that my mother had died. She had had a global stroke two months prior. The Lord had given me a dream to comfort and prepare me that she did not have a lot of life left in her.

I had tried to see her and had even booked a flight. But due to such a massive family with her own siblings themselves making up a crowd, my siblings told me to wait.

A few weeks before she passed away, my one brother paid for a plane ticket for me to go see her. That was huge since I didn't have a lot of money due to still paying bills. I got to spend 10 days pretty much alone with my mother, which reassured both of us of her commitment to Jesus as she had come to Him before her passing.

So that cold February morning, I got the call that Mom had gone to be with the Lord. I knew I did not have the money to go to the funeral.

I had spent the last few nights at my friend's place. She had insisted that I stay with her as she didn't want me to be alone. That was a gift from God since I didn't want to be alone knowing I couldn't be with Mom as she was taking her dying breaths. I was also thankful for the week-long visit I had with Mom the previous October.

Mom had seemed unusually quiet and very peaceful on that trip like I had never seen her before. All she wanted to do was play her favourite game. I recall looking across the table at her and asking the Lord if He was preparing me. She was 86.

It was 9:00 a.m. the morning of Mom's homegoing when I got the call from the bridal boutique. Could I come into work at 10:00 a.m.? I was desperately needing a job and knew I couldn't say no. I knew it would be a way to keep busy and to be strong 'til I could get to the funeral. I felt a deep peace from God to take the job.

I felt the Lord ministering to me there. That first day, it did not make sense that I was not falling apart with Mom's death. I had a peace that she and I both knew she was doing great, and she would have wanted me to take the job and be able to pay my bills.

The staff were all kind to me, and that first day, I only worked with my boss and sold a lot of dresses for her. She was amazed and told me at the end of the day that it was likely the busiest day of the year. She told me I brought peace to that place, and it had been so peaceful to work with me. That kept me from falling apart. It was a gift to both of us. I only told them my mom had died when it was time to go to the funeral.

I drove 18 hours one way through B.C. and the Rocky Mountains to get to northern Alberta for the funeral. I found out some of my siblings thought I shouldn't speak at the funeral—too much Jesus I carried maybe. I had to forgive again. At least Mom knew and my kids knew I had come to show my respect. That was all that counted in God's eyes.

A Bride Named Trinity

One day, I was rearranging some dresses. A bride walked in as they often do. The brides I found, for the most part, were quite delightful and happy. I mean, someone had chosen them to be their beloved, and as a bridal consultant, my job was to facilitate finding them a gown and accessories. And of course, my job was to always make it a wonderful memory for them too.

This one bride was quite unique. Her name was Trinity. Well, that caught my attention. I thought, *"God, today I'm dressing and preparing the Trinity?"*

She was such fun—so happy and eager to get married. She had only one request, an extremely different one from any other bride I had had the privilege to work with. Trinity was adamant she wanted a gold dress, loads of bling, and sequins. I mean gold, gold, gold. Nothing else would do for her wedding—not white, not ivory, but gold. It did not matter if the dress was heavy as some of those dresses weighed 25 to 30 lbs. (Yup, you got biceps when you lifted those dresses all day.)

I have often pondered what God was saying. I mean, I have known and had a revelation for years that God was not poor. He took me to Nashville in November of 1996, and I toured the TBN grounds and studio and saw the glory of God, and I knew He was not poor.

If we are the King's kids, perhaps He would like us to pay attention to His glory—that He Himself is clothed in majesty and splendor. Maybe He likes to show it off to His kids and the world. I have often said that if I was a king and had sons and daughters, I would like to show them off. If they always went around in rags and were paupers, would that reflect my kingdom and majesty?

I tell you one thing I learned from Trinity that day. She liked to display and put on the glory, and she certainly didn't mind the rest of us seeing her either.

A Bride Called Faith

One day, my boss got to work and immediately had us slash the prices on a bunch of wedding gowns, shoes, veils, and accessories. I had never seen this yet in my time there. When we were done replacing the sales tags to new 75% off tags, in walked a lovely bride-to-be. This bride's name was Faith.

Faith came in with her mom and grandmother. They were all very delightful and easy to please. I thought to myself, *"Okay, Lord, what do You want me to learn from Faith?"*

I filled in the usual bridal registry to get her information for the computer. Then, I wrote down her desires for her dress, where the wedding ceremony and reception would be held, etc.—all the usual stuff.

We went through the bridal shop selecting dresses to try along with veils and accessories. The three of them were delighted that we were having a huge sale. So, shoes off and into the bridal room we went to try everything on.

I had sold many dresses where the bride went back to the first gown she tried on. As a bridal consultant, you get to know the dresses and designers you carry as well as different figures. One does get to know what will look great on each shape, and trust me, there are a multitude of shapes.

Faith was a gem and a real joy. I think it was the first of the dresses, veils, and shoes she tried on that she said, "This is it. I'm saying yes to the dress."

I asked her if she had known about our sale. She said, "No."

Then I thought, *"Wait a minute! We as staff didn't even know about the sale 'til this morning."*

I was in awe. She was the first bride I had ever worked with that got her entire head-to-toe bridal wear—dress, veil, accessories, and shoes—for 75% off. She was even the first one to hit our sale. Her mom and grandma said Faith had gotten up that morning and said that she *had* to go look for a dress. We were the first place she came to.

Okay, now we were all surprised at how things worked out. It was so incredibly wonderful for Faith. Her mom or grandma piped up and said, "You know, Rhéa, life always works out this way for Faith. She always gets what she hopes for."

"Aha" moment right there, folks! It haunted me then and still does to this day. Perhaps I had been once again visited by the Glorious Trio released from on high. I won't know 'til I get to Heaven, but I did sense God's presence in that room as they spoke to me about how "Life always works this way for Faith. She always gets what she hopes for."

This is a word for all of us, I'm sure. Whatever you do, don't stop believing...for that is what faith does.

Chocolate Angel

While working at the bridal boutique, I had started a "Prayer for Canada" group at the church. God brought together an amazing group of faithful intercessors. We had a shared burden for our nation and a desire to see God's glory and Kingdom be brought to our land, to see His name become famous, and to have righteous rule again in our land. I was so thankful for these faithful intercessors who stood in the gap with me to pray.

One day at the bridal shop as I was helping a woman find a gown, I got a sudden tap on the shoulder from behind. As I turned around—and to my surprise—there was a curly-haired fellow wearing a cowboy hat. He was an elderly man who seemed really quite delighted with himself as he handed me a large chocolate butterfly. As he gave it to me, he said eagerly, "Enjoy the butterfly." Then, he turned and walked away.

I was stunned and surprised to say the least. The chocolate butterfly came from the chocolate boutique in the mall where I worked. They made fine and outta this world chocolates.

There I stood, holding a huge chocolate butterfly while serving a customer. She and I looked at each other and smiled. I shrugged my shoulders and asked if I could be excused to go to the back staff room where I set it on the lunch table.

I wasn't away very long before I was back serving the mother of the bride again when suddenly, another quick tap on the shoulder. There to my surprise was my new curly-haired friend with two chocolate maple leaves. He then said excitedly, "Enjoy the maple leaves." No sooner had he said that, then he turned and scooted off.

Now, I was even more puzzled and curious. Who was he? Why did he do this? I mean, we had never seen each other before. As I turned around, my customer was laughing. She could read my surprised attitude. I shrugged it off and again made my way to the staff room to set these new chocolates down on my now growing stash pile.

My co-workers in the back room were surprised and chuckling. We all thought it was funny. I secretly thought, *"Lord, what is this about?"*

A few days went by, and again, another visit from my new secret admirer. Again, he tapped me on the shoulder and said, "Enjoy the chocolates," and left. Now, I was at attention! The other girls at work all laughed and enjoyed watching this.

A few days later, it happened yet again. I was only working part-time, and it seemed he only came and delivered chocolates when I was there and only for me. The other gals insisted he never did it for them.

I shared the chocolates with the gals, and they enjoyed them with me, for I couldn't eat them all if I wanted to still fit into my dresses. I told the gals that perhaps his wife died, and it comforted him to do that for others.

He was a cute, little elderly man who had a lot of joy and a bounce in his step. Somehow, I was not creeped out by him. I did not sense he was hitting on me but had peace about receiving his kind and delicious gifts. These chocolates were also quite pricey, so they were enjoyed as a real specialty treat by all who tasted them.

He brought joy to my days and joy to the staff. One day as I was standing near the entrance of the shop, he walked up. Upon handing me a few beautifully wrapped chocolates, he began to explain that his wife had died 15 years earlier. Now, he loved to go around and bless people with chocolates because she loved chocolates, and he could no longer buy them for her. I was one of his chosen recipients.

How I marveled at that little man! He took a great sorrow, tragedy, and the lemons life had given him and made lemonade. I mean, he turned his tears into a chocolate encouragement ministry. He would just light up when he saw the surprise on my face each time he appeared.

I am not sure why I was chosen, but I do know that God wanted to show me His love and have some fun. God was comforting that man, me, and all my co-workers who benefited from his decadent gift-giving ministry.

How about us? Will we wallow in our self-pity and the pain of our past? Or will we pick ourselves up and dust ourselves off and go out and encourage others? That little fella was God's "Chocolate Angel" to me for a season of life.

I even recall those special chocolate maple leaves as though Holy Spirt was whispering, "I like it that you pray for Canada. Keep going, Rhéa, keep going."

The huge chocolate butterfly felt like God was saying to me, "You are getting your big wings. Now you are free. So, fly, Baby, fly."

"God, I live in a barn."

Circumstances can happen in life that you never think will ever happen to you. I went through a brutal divorce. While I do not care to go into the details of that here, I do want to share that there are some things that will happen in your life that you would never wish on your worst enemy.

Having fled an abusive relationship, I had to move every two months for a while. I did not know where to turn. There were hardly any rentals anywhere for the little money that I had, and I still had to buy gas and groceries.

A gal I knew had an old quonset. It was an old 100-year-old mechanical shop. It was dome shaped, and I decided, perhaps, I may have to live there. To put it quite simply, it was as far from the Ritz-Carlton hotels as you could get!

I chatted with the owner. She was very hesitant to rent it to me. She said it had no running water, bathroom, toilet, and barely a kitchen. She did not want to be known as a slum landlord. A year before, she had rented it to a man who stayed there for a bit. She could not believe a woman was that desperate for a roof over her head. I told her I was. We chatted, and she agreed to rent it to me.

I still recall secretly hoping a mouse would not fall into my mouth while I slept in the loft upstairs. But God sent me a blessing. Another friend saw the place and said, "Rhéa, you wait here." That very first night, she brought bed sheets and fabric. We stapled them to the tin foil above my new curtain ceiling for a roof over my bed. There were tons of mouse holes, rips, and tears in that roof. The mice liked the old insulation.

That first night, I remember being exhausted from soooo many moves over the past few months. As I sat on the edge of that twin bed, I remember looking up and saying sadly, "God, I live in a barn."

He instantly spoke to my heart and said, "Rhéa, I know what it's like to live in a stable."

With that said, I began to laugh. I asked Him, "God are you trying to stabilize me?" I laughed and said, "Yes, God, you did live in a barn-like stable."

As I lay there that night and every night for a long time after, I saw eight golden lions walking around my bed each night. I felt safe somehow...even though I did have to lock the door with a rope the size of my pinky finger and tie it to the roof.

Jesus had endured, so I could endure. It helped me to be reminded of that as I cleaned mountains and piles and piles of mouse droppings. It helped me to remember that as I lived with the old oil smell from vehicles and machinery that were once fixed in that shop.

We had a lot of rain that summer. Up in the loft, it would get so hot and humid from the rain that poured down the sides of the brick chimney. The insulation by my bed should have been pink, but after decades of being there, it had turned black. So, my girlfriend came and covered that with plastic wrap.

I realized I was not alone and had a roommate in the basement. A salamander lived a lonely existence down there. I hoped he didn't get drowned by the rain in the flooded basement.

With no toilet or running water, I told God that He would have to show me that He was Lord of my body. And He did. Every time I needed a washroom, I was at one of my three girlfriends' houses. They also generously opened their homes so that I could shower. Yup, as a woman with no toilet, God indeed showed me that He was Lord of my body.

I learned to cultivate His presence more there and would start the day with worship and dancing after reading the Word. God's presence would come, and I felt He delighted in me making a lemonade dance outta the lemons I had been given. For you see, He, too, learnt to be content and soothed in a stable.

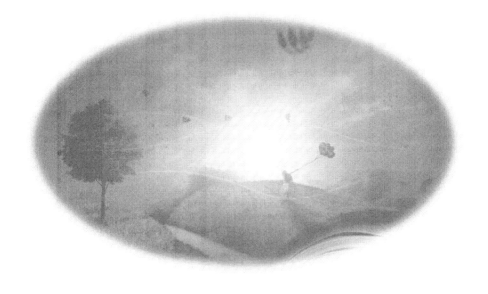

From Garden of Weedin' to Garden of Eden

My girlfriend—the one who had hung the bed sheets and fabric over my bed and had me over a countless number of times for tea and meals and saw me cry so much—was a dear comfort. My pastors at the time also had me over for tea and meals. This was God's greatest gift in my heartache...to be in other people's beautiful homes.

I had left behind more than 40 different homes. Several moves were due to being an oil patch wife. They transferred families often. Then, we had the house fire and went through five moves that year. We had also renovated homes and flipped them. So, to end up in this old quonset sorta took the cake. I had lived in modest homes and luxury homes, but this was the shack of them all.

My friend said one day, "Rhéa, you need to open an art gallery and sell your art."

I had run a gallery for a friend in a small town for almost two years and sold some of my art as well as other artists' art. People from all over the world came to that little town. They had a beautiful little town—quaint with a very old-fashioned theatre and hospitality. I was exhausted but knew she was right.

Another girlfriend who had me stay with her when I had nowhere to live took me to Value Village, a secondhand store. I had lived with her twice for six months each time, making up a year of being roommates. We just "got" each other, sharing some crazy life situations that other people simply did not get. I knew she had incredible taste, and we both loved to decorate. So, off we went with my last $200.00.

Well, we had been to a service that morning, and the pastor had anointed us with oil. I think he poured half a jar on top of each of our heads!

So, here we were shopping for fabrics to hang over shelving, drape over cupboards, and staple onto ceilings. To our surprise, we noticed people staring at us. We thought perhaps it was due to us having two heaping carts full of fabrics, vases, and flowers.

As we got to the till ready to pay for our overflowing carts, we realized they were probably staring at our greasy hair as much as our carts! We had a belly laugh leaving that store.

So, off I went. I worked long days and painted a lot of wood, walls, and pinned up fabrics. My pastors and a couple of friends came to help me. My pastor built some steps for me. I hung curtains after I painted the window where the mushrooms grew inside where the rain had leaked in.

After two weeks of hard work, I opened my gallery. My one friend was a professional set painter for theatre and surprised me by painting me a gorgeous outdoor sign—Rhéa Sunshine Art Gallery. It had a huge sunflower on it. I painted the front door the same color with a huge sunflower on it, and "ta da!"—I was open for business!

God fed me through the sales of my art. On the first day I opened the door, the first people who walked in were from Australia, then Bulgaria, India, Germany, Scotland, etc. The nations came to my transformed barn/stable. Many signed my guest book.

They were in awe and so was I. God had taken a burnt-out, broken-down Jesus girl and helped her know she could have her own business, and He would bless her and feed her. I had folks who just liked to come there and sit in the presence of God.

God knows where you are. He will make a way. You just have to put your hand to the plow and obey.

Someone even wrote in my guest book: "It's like walking into the Garden of Eden."

Sometimes, you will feel like Cinderella. Life's not fair. You had it all, lost it all, feel like a slave cleaning someone else's mess… but God sees you, sweetheart. You are not alone. If you get yourself still enough, you will feel His every breath and every move. He is there, and He cares.

And one day—when the time is right—you will be like Joseph and Cinderella. You will be taken from the prison to the palace. Don't lose heart!

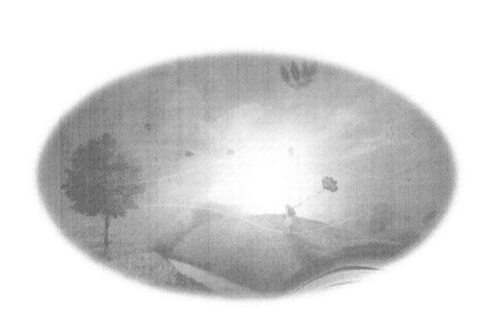

Moving to Kelowna

In August of 2014, I moved to Kelowna, British Columbia (BC).

Nine times, I had been given words to lay my family on the altar. The eighth word came from my pastor. He also said God would take me somewhere hot and sunny.

I knew it was Kelowna. I had had a vision and dreams of me living in that city about 12 years before. Now was the time.

God has a way of getting you outta your comfort zone. He really does! I had finally gotten an apartment in Calgary. I was trying to make it on my own. I finally had a home where I could have my kids over to my place for a Christmas dinner.

For four years before that, I had had to meet them in restaurants for Christmas, Easter, Thanksgiving, etc. or in my children's homes. We would only be able to visit for a couple of hours. Not exactly the way a little girl dreams it should be, right? I mean, the mom should have the home, kitchen, cook the turkey and trimmings, decorate the tree, but I really had no home.

I had fled my home often for many years to escape the anger and verbal abuse and would shake inside all the time. I was a wreck and tired of the lies.

My friends had told me to keep a night bag packed all the time in my jeep. I was thankful for that advice. Finally, tired of fleeing night after night and not knowing where I would sleep, I left for my own sanity. My youngest was 18.

I severely overprotected my kids and never let them know what was going on. My ex would save his outbursts for when they were not home. Checking into hotels at midnight and staying at my sister's became common. One night, I even drove to another city and slept in my vehicle at a truck stop. I felt afraid and very alone.

I finally got an apartment and thought I would make it. To my horror, there turned out to be drug dealers living upstairs, and one night, I woke up to a party of about 40 men upstairs. I was the only woman downstairs. I had to put boxes and bins in front of the door that divided us. I awoke to that huge party and a chair crashing on the floor upstairs over my bed.

God had given me a dream that I would need to lock myself in the bathroom and pray all night. It happened, and I did. I grabbed a candle, lit it, and prayed much of that night.

The next morning, I awoke to a loud shout of someone demanding their money and threatening to beat someone up. They kept threatening to kill the young 20-year-old drug dealer who had just moved in.

My friends all said that I *had* to get out. So, now I had a midnight move on my resume. I had to flee again.

A friend took me in again. We had special times and healing times. God bonded us so that we could travel together in future days. We motivated each other to write our books.

All along, God was working to get me to Kelowna. Helped through the sweat, labour, and love of friends, my kids, and my church, God helped me move.

One of those friends worked so hard to move me during those times along with the others. She worked like a man, moving me, and driving my truck. My friends also helped me to unpack. For the first two months, I was so exhausted, God just had me soak.

I had kind of missed the whole "soaking" movement. Perhaps, I had internally judged it. I mean, friends would laugh. They would try to get me to soak, but I couldn't. I'd lay there with one eye open. I mean, seriously, I was always the kind that was like, "God, if You are gonna move or do something, I do *not* want to miss it."

I was definitely a non-soaker on purpose. I mean, I didn't make a sign or placard and protest, but internally, I protested. I thought, *"Great! Now we have all these people laying around like couch potatoes on floors and couches 'soaking' while all their neighbours are going straight to hell."* So, I thought, *"Enough of creating a culture of couch potatoes! I am a mover and a shaker...literally."* (If you are not convinced, then reread my stories.)

When I arrived in Kelowna, due to the spiritual climate, God forced me to soak. For two months, I could do nothing else. He will show you one way or another.

I found out soaking has benefits. I'm not by any means a regular or professional soaker. Maybe, I do it my own way. Perhaps, I soak as I can. I think I do. It's called soaking-on-the-way.

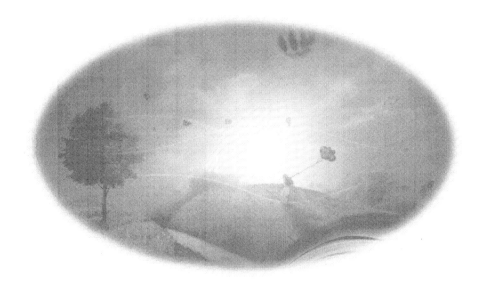

Jesus at a Soup Kitchen

After two months of soaking and being still, a friend suggested I call her friend, Kenny[6]. Kenny worked at the downtown soup kitchen, the Kelowna Gospel Mission.

I met Kenny, and he invited me to go there to sit and eat with the homeless and join their Bible study. The first time I went down there, I told another person who had invited me, "Don't you leave me alone in this place."

I literally saw so many people there demonically manifesting. I thought, *"Goodness! They all have a legion."* I had forgotten my authority after years of fleeing abusive situations.

Kenny reminded me that we bring peace in when we walk in the door. I brought a friend, and she, too, reminded me of who I was in Christ as we sat and ate with them all there.

Jesus would give them dreams at night, and they would line up in the early morning and ask Kenny how to get saved. We started a homeless home group and saw cancer healed and deaf ears opened. We saw addicts get delivered and get their own apartments. God was on the move!

One day, I sat across from a particular man. He had long hair and beautiful eyes. He was new there. The fellow on my left ate with a large screwdriver by his plate. The fellow on my right had fallen

---

[6] Name changed to protect privacy

asleep or passed out in his plate. The couple across from me were fighting and yelling at me. Wow!

This new fellow...well, he brought peace. I asked him his name and where he was from—just small talk. I didn't really know what to do, so I thought I could ask him what his dream life would be. I mean, if he could do anything, what would he love to do?

He looked at me quietly and tenderly. He told me he had travelled from city to city and loved to tell others of Jesus as he stayed on the streets. Then, he was quiet for a few moments.

Suddenly, he said very thoughtfully as he took a bite of bread, "What would I do if I could do anything?"

"This is it," he answered confidently with great love and assurance. As he said this, he spread his arms out wide and said, "This is it."

I almost dropped my soup spoon full of soup. "This is it?" I questioned.

Internally, I thought, *"Are you kidding me? I mean, buddy, just tell me anything, and I can pray you outta it and into the new."* You cannot imagine my shock at his unspeakable delight in doing what he was doing and even feeling called to do it.

I was speechless, and that for me, folks, is no small miracle! I mean, who was this guy who could bring a hush to a chaotic supper table in a volatile environment? Wow, I was undone. Could this be my Lord? An angel? I somehow knew he was not an ordinary man.

He later came to Bible study and sat outside our circle but kind of behind where I was sitting. I could look back and see him. He was very quiet throughout our discussions. He did not seem disturbed that the addicts would be normal one minute and go outside for five minutes and come back in, high on heroin or crack.

He observed, he listened, he brought peace. Could we have been visited by the Prince of Peace? Heaven only knows, but I did breathe in something about my Lord that night in that soup kitchen.

The Greatest Invitation

I just wanted to take some time here to tell you about eternity. Heaven is real and so is eternity. In fact, eternity is forever.

Where will *you* spend it?

It's a really big question, but it's one that I challenge you to consider. Hell is real also. Personally, I have chosen Heaven as my destination.

Many folks spend a lifetime planning for this life—where to live, raise a family, work, retire, etc. Not many people think about when their heartrate monitor stops, or the graveyard digger starts digging their grave 6 feet under. Seriously, folks! That is not a great time to think about and decide where you will go as you will already likely be there...either in a place you *want* to be or in a place you would *not* want your worst enemy to be.

If you choose Heaven, then you need to choose to invite the Maker of Heaven into your heart. I can help you, and it's easier than you think.

Go ahead and pray this prayer and mean it. Take it seriously.

> "Jesus, I realize I am a sinner. Please forgive me of my sins and come and live inside my heart. Have dominion of my life, Lord. Amen!"

If you said this prayer, then congratulations! You have reserved yourself the finest spot to spend eternity. You will never regret it.

I also encourage you to pray, get a Bible, and read it daily. This will help you to know Jesus better. Also, find a good Bible-believing church near you where you can belong to a family of believers that will help you to grow on your new journey.

Nation Quakers

On March 2nd of 2019 as I sat in a Saturday evening service, I had a vision. In the vision, people were climbing a mountain. They were very tired as their enemy had put a bunch of boulders in their path. These boulders made their climb and progress up the mountain more difficult. The boulders were meant to hinder their progress of ascending the mountain.

Jesus came and started to remove some boulders. As the people saw Him doing this, they began to laugh. As they laughed, I saw the Lord begin to remove more boulders. The more they laughed, the more boulders He seemed to remove.

Joy was being renewed, and many were receiving new strength for the journey. It did seem as though the Lord and the people were enjoying this reality, for as the Word says, the joy of the Lord is our strength[7].

Suddenly, they were at the top of the mountain. They had made it! They rested a bit, and then the Lord turned and faced the other side of the mountain. He waved and motioned for them to come and follow Him once more.

There was a large slide, and He was the first to go down. As He did this, others felt safe to follow, and so down the slide they went. The slide landed in a beautiful, refreshing pool of water. In the bottom of the pool were beautiful, precious stones and

---

[7] See Nehemiah 8:10

jewels. Some of the stones and jewels had letters on them. Some had words like 'overcomer', 'victorious', etc.

Jesus picked up the 'overcomer' stones, and He began to fashion and string necklaces out of these. He said, "These are for the overcomers, as they have overcome so much." He then handed those out.

I then saw Him pick up individual letter stones and string new necklaces. I saw the words "Nation Quakers" on these freshly made ones. I recall being surprised and actually thinking, *"Nation Quakers? Hmmm."* He then handed these out to some folks in the pool.

I shared this vision that night. Within 24 hours, friends called and said there had been 3 earthquakes. One was in Rocky Mountain House, Alberta (AB), and was a 4.3. Another followed in Red Deer, AB, and was a 4.6. The 3rd one I heard of was a 2.2 in Salmon Arm, BC. The first 2 were fairly large for quakes happening where they had not been recorded before.

The Lord confirmed that vision quite quickly. I think that perhaps some folks from Alberta and BC got these Nation Quaker necklaces.

I am not usually a storm chaser, except for a few years back when I jumped in the backseat of car full of young gals who were going to chase a tornado. I had peace about it. We had tornado warnings, but I had seen and lived through a deadly tornado and knew this one was fairly big but not deadly. The skies were really beautiful on that night, and we did pray. It ceased its manifestation before it could grow larger.

Somehow, the Lord prompted me to start watching earthquake activities when I lived in BC. I had felt a 4.2 in my building as I lived on the second floor. I was at the elevator and there was a loud bang. It shook the whole floor, and if you were in the elevator, you would have caught air. I had checked the clock on my stove before I headed out the door and it was 9:26 a.m. The elevator was right across from my apartment. I pressed the elevator button at 9:28 a.m., and that was when I heard the loud boom. The next day, the newspaper said an earthquake had hit at 9:28 a.m. I was also watching global quakes at the same time as being prompted to check things out in BC.

I'm still in awe of how quickly the Lord confirmed the above quakes. It proves He is a mover and a shaker. People, get ready...cuz there will be a whole lot of shaking going on! The Word tells us so.

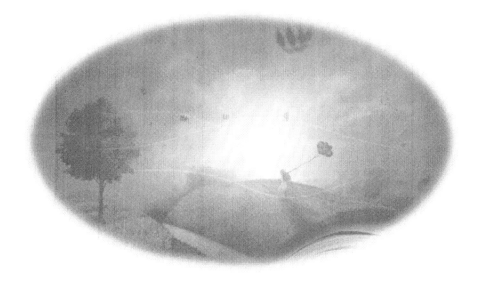

Three Ambulance Rides

in a Decade

This is perhaps the most difficult to write about. I'm not sure why, but I even pondered whether to put it in my book or not. After discussing it with few friends, they thought it was quite important. They considered it a big part of my overcoming journey. I was advised to be brave and tell this part of my story.

For most of my life, I have enjoyed excellent health. My mother told me that I had scarlet fever twice as a child, but other than that, I was always in good health. So, this next part kind of took the cake so to speak.

You see, when you are normally very active and an on-the-go type of person like I have been, you are not used to sitting around. For sure, you are not used to life being put on pause. As I write this part out, I guess that I am still realizing this has been a big part of my broken wing journey.

Perhaps I was disappointed in myself and thought maybe my faith was not where it needed to be at the time. During this period of my journey, I did not feel like God's woman of faith and power but like I was God's woman of "paste and flour." Yup, for real. I was declaring and believing and standing on the Word but not seeing a lot shifting in the natural or with pain levels. I needed a lot of grace during these times.

Anyways, here goes as I try to share some of these fiery trials, as I had to relearn how to walk again 3 times in my life.

Ambulance Ride #1

In the summer of 2006, I began to hemorrhage. It was bad and went on for 6 weeks. I somehow felt like the woman with the issue of blood I had read about in the Bible. It was so bad that friends had to pray that I would make it down the aisle without blood everywhere at a family member's wedding. (Sorry for too much info here, but that was seriously how it was.) During that time, I was so weak and had lost so much blood that my skin was very white.

I was scheduled to go to a conference where I was going to introduce some folks. After the meeting, we went out for a bite to eat. One of the prophets at the table noticed that there was something unusual about the server.

We ordered our food and said grace when the food arrived. I reached for a chicken wing and bit into it...and immediately took it out of my mouth saying as I recall, "That's wicked!"

I knew something was wrong as an evil smell hit my nose as I bit into that wing. I did not chew or swallow it and took it out of my mouth. My young friend at the table said, "Rhéa, are you okay?"

I said, "Pray for me."

And I guess I passed out. Apparently, my body fell out of the booth and onto the floor. My friends said that I landed really badly on my ankle.

My girlfriend and her daughter started yelling in tongues really loudly, so loudly that it cleared out that packed out restaurant.

They sat me up, and I passed out again, falling badly on my ankle again. They told me that I passed out 3 times.

We finally got to the bathroom, and I recall my girlfriend holding my head in her lap on the bathroom floor while her daughter kept saying, "Stay with me, Rhéa, stay with me."

She told me later that, 3 times when she was saying that over me as I was in and out of consciousness, my eyes had turned sapphire blue. I had heard that the Throne of God was made of emeralds and sapphires. So, I told her that was Jesus on the inside of me fighting for me as I had told Him earlier that day that I was tired of the fight.

Two paramedics came into the washroom and ordered an ambulance. They had been placed in the restaurant by God that night. Interestingly, they did not get scared away by my friends yelling in tongues. They were the only ones who stayed. They could have even been angels. Angels would not have been afraid of folks yelling in tongues. Only God knows who they were, but they were a big help.

Off I went in the ambulance.

Later, I asked the doctor in the wee hours of the morning if I had been poisoned. She said yes and that, if I had swallowed that bite of chicken wing, I would have died, for it had been soaked in a very toxic chemical.

I had noticed that when I bit into that wing, it had a very wicked smell, and the meat inside was a very dark grey. While I do not want to give glory to the devil, this was witchcraft. I heard afterwards that there had been other episodes at that place, and they shut down shortly afterwards.

The devil hits you when you are weak. Remember, I had just been hemorrhaging, and now this happened on top of that.

The church needs to know about this stuff. It's real! The Word says, *"My people are destroyed for lack of knowledge..."* (Hosea 4:6)

The long-term effect of this incident was not walking for 6 months due to severely damaged tendons and ligaments in my ankle due to how I fell.

At the end of 6 months, I remember going to my easel one day to paint. I was painting a worship dancer. She was bowed down in adoration. All of a sudden, I felt someone grab my brush, and I began to paint feet. To my surprise, a perfect foot appeared. I gasped as I had never painted feet before not to mention a perfect one. There was no way that I painted that foot by myself. Jesus or an angel must have grabbed my brush as I have had that happen on a few occasions before.

There was an "awe" moment as I felt like God wanted to give me a visual that I would walk again since I was losing hope. I was speechless and awestruck once more. That filled me with such faith and hope that I, too, would walk and dance again.

Within a very short time, I was off those crutches and healed on time to make Christmas Eve dinner. That, my friends, was no small miracle!

So, I say once again... Thank you, Lord!

Ambulance Ride #2

I will skip ambulance ride number 2 for time's sake, but I tore my IT band and could not walk for another 6 months. I had to relearn to walk all over again.

Ambulance Ride #3

Yes, I'm serious, and yes, this really happened! This 3rd time around, I told the Lord, "I cannot go through this again."

It was about 3:00 o'clock on a lovely March day. I was going upstairs, and my IT band snapped. For those who do not know what an IT band is, it is a large, elastic-like band on the side of your outer thigh. If it snaps or tears, you instantly cannot walk. You will either fall forwards or backwards but literally cannot move or walk. Apparently, it is very rare but usually happens to female marathon runners. I had never run marathons except in the spirit.

This all happened at the top of my stairs. It was a miracle I did not fall down the stairs and had my phone on me. I called my girlfriend who was home at the time. Another miracle... She came right away and ordered an ambulance. I still do not recall how I got down the stairs and into my favourite chair.

So, off I went in the ambulance, sirens and all. I could not believe it. Like, aren't ambulances for heart attacks and strokes? Serious stuff, right? Not legs, right? But here I was again. Well, I was about to learn how serious this would be.

The doctor who saw me asked if I had heard a loud snap or pop. My reply was, "I think the whole block could hear it!" I mean, when you tear your IT band, it snaps *very* loudly. The doctor knew right away what it was.

Yes, you guessed it. My IT band had torn, this time on the other leg. He then said that this was way more painful than if you break a bone. I already knew that from past experience. He said that it also took way longer to heal than a broken bone.

Well, I had the Lord and the Word and over 60 healing Scriptures to stand on, so I would be declaring and decreeing, but this time, my faith took a really big hit. I did not realize 'til a bit later how big a hit this was being as it was the 3rd accident.

Why me? Could I even endure another 6 months go around if it lasted that long again? I had some serious questions.

For the first 9 to 10 months, I spent all day on the couch with 5 pillows or so under my knee. As a child, I had seen a cartoon of a person in the hospital with their foot in a sling or rope that hung from the ceiling. I so felt like that cartoon character! But this was real life, and this was me. No joke, right? I could hardly believe it.

For those first 9 months, I had to sleep with huge, doubled-up ice cooler packs under each knee. My other knee was sore as it had been damaged before and now had to carry all my weight. Taking 3 extra strength Advil did nothing to take away the pain. I was confessing Isaiah 53:3-5, Psalms 103, and 1 Peter 2:24, confessing I was healed while in unbelievable amounts of physical pain.

Forty-five faithful friends came to care for me. They were a bunch of intercessors that I had worked with in the city. The Lord would tell some of them to come by the house to open my blinds or that I needed a cup of tea. They brought groceries and meals and comfort to me. This was living proof that we are meant to live in community and be there for one another, right?

Some gals came over to wash my hair for me. We would prop up a bunch of cushions on a dining room chair. They would drag the chair to the kitchen sink. I would hobble over, and they would wash my hair in the kitchen sink while we laughed at how crazy this all was. Thank the Lord for faithful friends!

I had a couple of male friends who would pick me up for doctor's appointments. I would have to go up the stairs on my backside, and we would all count to 3 and they would hoist me up under my arms carefully and hand me crutches to get to the car. They kindly waited for my appointments to be over, and then we would grab a bucket of chicken and salads and go for a picnic by the water as these were my only few outings.

It would have been nice to say I was able to walk in 6 months this time, but that was not the case. This was the worst of them all. For outings, my girlfriend brought a wheelchair to wheel me around in. My total recovery time was almost 3.5 years. At the time of this writing, it has only been in the past few weeks where I have slept with no pain in my legs. My legs often literally felt like they were on fire the whole time.

Six months into this last accident, I got a call from a prayer line that I had contacted. When the intercessor heard about my situation, she began to weep. She wept for about half an hour. This woman understood as she had had the same thing happen to her. She understood the extreme pain involved, and it caused her to weep for me. She said it took her 10 months to walk again.

Knowing that someone else understood allowed me to weep a bit. It was actually like the Lord saying, "I see you, Rhéa, and I understand."

Now, it's not rocket science to ask the Lord questions, right? So, about a few months into things this time, I said, "God, what is going on? I love You and totally live for You. I believe in healing, etc."

His reply was not what I expected. He said, "Rhéa, I want you to write down all the leg accidents you know of in your family."

So, I began to write. At the last count that I knew of, there were 44 leg accidents from broken legs, ankles, injured knees, etc. My sister even had a horse fall on her leg while out riding. You see, I knew the devil was (and is) a legalist, and now it was being highlighted to me that this was part of a cycle of generational curses. God, help us! I also felt that it was witchcraft mixed with a generational curse.

People actually pray things like, "God bring so-and-so to their knees." That, my friends, is nothing but witchcraft. Jesus Himself never once prayed that way, and you could be cursing folks if you do so. Be careful and be wise. You would never want someone to pray that for you.

Yes, the Word says we are redeemed from the law of sin and death, but it also says in the same Bible that, *"My people are destroyed for lack of knowledge."* (Hosea 4:6) Sometimes, you have got to get to the root of things.

I certainly did see that there was a pattern playing out in my life that I wanted to get rid of. I sensed the devil had a legal right due to something my ancestors had done. I am still waiting for the fullness of that revelation as we are all in process. If you are certain that you have this all figured out, let me know. I'm always up to learning. What the world does not need more of, though, in cases like this are people like Job's friends.

All I know for sure is that, for my whole life, the enemy of our souls has been trying to take me out as he has likely been trying to take you out also. It's been a wild ride!

The Bible says, *"...having done all...stand."* (Ephesians 6:13) And I literally could not walk never mind stand for over 4 years of my life. The devil would say, "Look at you! You can't stand. You can't even walk and will never walk again and never dance again."

Dance is one of my primary ways to worship, so that was a bit much. He would taunt me and say, "Look, you are even in a wheelchair," which I was, even at airports. Somehow, he tried to put shame on me for not being able to stand on my own two feet.

It was an experience with how folks looked at me in the wheelchair. Some looked at me with pity, some looked down at me, some stared and wondered, *"What's up with that?"* Some looked away as they didn't know what to say or do. Most, I found, were kind.

I found it challenging since I knew my legs should cooperate and function normally...but they did not. I remember thinking I should have been instantly healed as I had seen so many times before. "Normal" just seemed to be a setting on a dryer as I once heard someone say.

My faith was really tested and so was my trust in God. I somehow miraculously never blamed Him, but I did a few times have to deal with disappointment that things were not changing. I just had to trust the whole time that tomorrow would be a better day.

Now, here I am after all this time, and guess what, devil? I'M STILL STANDING!

It may feel at times like your life is not fair. It may feel at times like you just cannot go on another day. I can honestly say that I get that. But hang on! Continue to do all you know how to do. Keep on believing and trusting God through the process and when things do not make sense. Declare and decree anyways. Praise Him anyways. Victory will come to you somehow, and I am living proof of that.

God does not expect us to have it all together. In this part of my story, I felt like a train wreck, but He was faithful in sending me wonderful folks to care for and look after me and let me know that I was not alone. He will be there for you too.

Yes, my friend, even in times when you feel like your faith has been eroded, you will look back and see how He was faithful. Victory is in store for the upright. No matter what has happened, I still believe that healing is for us today! Some healings in the Bible were instant and some were that they got healed as they went. Stay in faith as there is a miracle coming to you somehow.

God Wants Out of the Box

I am really sensing that God wants me to tell you that He really wants out of your boxes. He wants out of your religious systems and its way of doing things.

As a parent, you speak to all your children differently depending on what they need and what would be helpful to them. I have found that, in different seasons, God has spoken to me differently. At times, He's used the still small voice, the Word, an audible voice, angels, license plates, cashiers, strangers, and even children.

Like, someone may say, "Hey, don't take that road." If you do not listen, you may find yourself in an accident or a bridge is closed, etc. Recently, I even had a fortune cookie say, "Use your talents as that is what they were created for." I felt like God put that message there for me that day.

Several years ago, He prompted me to move to another city. He gave me several words through people as well. Then, I was prompted by His whisper to go much sooner than I had planned. So, I packed my vehicle and headed out.

I was driving through the Rocky Mountains, and suddenly, my jeep began to rumble and shake. I thought, *"Oh, this does not sound good."* I began to take authority over it and commanded it to function properly in Jesus' name. It stopped shaking and resumed running normally. At that moment, I saw a large ram appear on the side of the road and knew, like Abraham, that all would be well.

151

Upon getting to a friend's place, I could not sleep, so I prayed in tongues all night. In the morning, the Lord said to go downtown and sit at a certain café. I had told Him in the night that I needed a place to stay, to which He replied, "Don't worry. I will bring them." I knew he meant the folks I would be staying with.

Now remember, I was in a new place and did not really know anyone except my lone friends, so I knew He had something up His sleeve. My friends had graciously offered to let me to stay with them, but I sensed the Lord wanted me to have my own place.

As I was enjoying a nice cup of coffee in the café and watching all the folks coming in, I was eager to meet my new divine appointment. Several people came in. Folks were friendly, and almost everyone said hello. All of a sudden, this couple walked in. They appeared to be happy, and they walked over to my table. The man slapped his hands on the table and said loudly, "This is God's country!"

Well, that got my attention. I said, "Oh, are you believers?"

He said, "Yes."

I invited them to come and join me for breakfast. We had a nice visit, and he said, "Where will you be staying?"

I said, "God told me He will bring the folks who have my place." They were as amazed as I was.

Then, he said to his wife, "Why don't we rent her our suite?"

We chatted, and they asked if I would like to look at it. Next thing I knew, I was in a van with folks that I had just met and going to see my new place. I just knew it was a God set-up...and it was!

You see, for a month before I left home to come out there, I had seen 3 names on license plates. When God does that, I usually know I will meet the people whose names I have seen on these. So, when I asked them their names, the couple had 2 of the names I had seen on license plates the month before. When we got to their house, you cannot imagine my surprise when they introduced their dog, and he had the 3rd name I had seen. Yes, this was no small miracle, and God had already prepared me to meet them, but it also took my obedience to listen to the voice of God to get there.

God is soooo good. He used that place to bring a lot of healing into my life through beauty and nature and, yes, He even used the dog. He gave me a beautiful home overlooking the lake and mountains and, yes, even my own swimming pool too. It pays to obey God!!

Caught in a Canadian Court System

It's crazy, but it's true, but while I was fighting to stand and walk on my own two feet, I was also trying to stand against injustice in that very same decade. This ordeal went on for almost a decade too. Never would I have dreamt to be there, but there I was.

There was a swirl of demonic stuff in there that was unreal. I had intercessors from different nations who would call the night before court, and all would give me the exact same word.

That place, my friends, was not for the faint in heart. I told many folks that this system was an animal to be tamed. You simply cannot face a giant like that in your own strength. I had to rely on God's strength and grace for every word.

Many times, I was amazed at what came out of my mouth and so were the judges and lawyers. I cannot go into all the details of that here now, but I am forever in awe of how God showed up.

In every movie I have seen of folks going to court, they always went with family or friends. I did not have that luxury. Everyone I knew was working, and I faced this mountain with my God alone walking in with me.

I learnt a lot. I saw a lot of injustice. I saw abuse. Somehow, I know that I took a forerunner hit for what many believers will go through in these last days. Jesus said, "You will be dragged before them, accused unjustly, etc. Be prepared as it will happen."

The Lord had me confront a wicked judge. I sent an email to this individual who was extremely abusive to me. The email went like this:

Dear Judge "So-and-So",

I found a verse in a very famous book that says, "Woe to you dishonest judges who continually rape widows and orphans." Do you know that folks can drag processes on to emotionally and financially rape you? This is very unjust to the Lord, and He takes it quite seriously. He hates dishonest measures and scales as it says in Proverbs. He is about to do a cleanup in these systems and the business world I have been sensing and told. Many prophets are saying this now. You see, God has seen who has lost much and who wants to take advantages of them, and He takes really good notes.

The above email resulted in this judge actually treating me like a human being after I sent that. That was a form of justice. If I would not have confronted them, they may have continued delaying things to keep getting their pocketbooks lined.

God told me when He visited me face to face that I would warn many, and this had to happen again. He showed me it would bring the fear of God which is increasing in our land more and more. I have heard of 18 people who died as a result of folks speaking against me. It was certainly not because I am so wonderful, but God knows who has been in the Throne Room with Him is all I can say.

One gal would kiss me on the cheek when she saw me and in front of all the others, but God showed me in a dream what she was doing behind my back. I felt like her kisses on my cheek were fake and similar to the Judas kiss that Jesus had gotten. About 2 years later, she lost 8 family members through death in all types of ways, one after another. I had to pray, "God, stop the plaque!" twice as this happened to another gal who also had been very abusive to me. These 2 gals each lost 7 to 8 family members. Yes, for real! Not fun! That still saddens me. Two other women mocked and laughed at a prophetic word I had given. They both died of cancer 2 years later. Again, I was grieved when I found out they had died.

If folks do crazy stuff behind my back, the Lord will show me who and what they are doing in dreams, and then He quietly tells me, "Just watch how their life goes now." It has not been pretty, and I certainly do not rejoice in it as it makes me quite sad.

People, get ready, for the fear of the Lord is coming, and the Lion is beginning to roar throughout the earth as never before. Warning here... If you have not walked a mile in someone's shoes or paid the price they have paid, refrain from speaking against them. No more casualties! It's time we get our hearts and mouths right before the Lord. The holy fear of God is coming back whether we like it or not.

Hit by a Mack Truck

I woke up at 3:00 a.m. that morning. Somehow that wasn't an uncommon time for me to pray, but on this particular morning, I sensed someone was in heavy-duty danger. I spent a whole hour pleading the blood of Jesus over everyone I knew of and myself.

There was this prophetic urgency, a warning that something bad was about to happen to someone. The Lord sometimes shows me who it is. He did not tell me that it would be me that day...but I was about to find out.

This part of this story is ALL about the power of the blood of Jesus. Yes, I want to brag about that! It saved my life numerous times and would do so again on that day as you are about to find out. I do not in any way think I would have survived totally uninjured and able to sleep in my own bed again that night had I not pleaded the blood of Jesus over myself and others. It is only because of this that I lived to talk about it. So, here goes...

Later that morning as I was finishing some errands, I decided to take another way home. I pulled up to a 3-way stop sign. On my right was a large semi-truck and trailer. The driver was yelling, but I could not hear him. There was a woman parked behind me in her car, so I could not back up either.

The driver of the semi-truck proceeded to turn but did not take his turn wide enough. He and I both knew he would hit me. Sure enough, he hit me. Then to my amazement, he stopped the semi, restarted it, backed it up, and hit me again after which I heard a loud crunch. Again, he stopped the monstrous truck and started it up again, backed up, and hit me for the 3rd time, and then I was yelling, "Stop already! You already hit me!"

Now I was thinking, *"Seriously, dude!"* Like, what was up with that?

He came to my window, and we exchanged information. I said, "You knew you were going to hit me, and you still hit me!"

I then asked him, "How old are you anyway?"

He said, "23."

I then asked how long he had been driving a semi. His reply was, "3 months."

Wow, now I saw that we had a novice driving a ton of weight that he was not sure how to handle. Things surely could have gone from bad to worse. Realizing he was also young, I told him, "Well, I have compassion for you," shaking my head.

He apologized, and then Holy Spirit prompted me by saying, "Tell him about Me."

I said, "Lord, I am not too happy with him right now."

The Lord again nudged me to tell him about Him, to which I replied, "Lord, this is not a good time."

Well, if you know Holy Spirit, He can be persistent. He knew what this young man and I both needed. So, yes, you guessed it. I was prompted again by the Trinity for the 3rd time to tell him about the Lord.

Now, I realized I had to switch gears and eat humble pie to carry this out. I was thinking, *"God, this is awkward, but here goes."*

Out of my mouth came my usual line, "Hey, has anyone ever told you that Jesus Christ loves you?"

He said, "No."

Now, I was the one feeling bad cuz I knew that, had I had died that morning, I would have been in eternity. But if something had happened to him, he would have never been told of this wonderful love, right? He would have never heard of my Saviour or that there even was one.

I said, "Well, He loves you, and He is way nicer than I am right now, and He is not even mad at you." He then thanked me, and we both went on our way.

Wow, God! I was humbled, safe, and alive...and he was enlightened.

Still now, I am in awe of not being killed or even injured. If he would have hit me a few inches over, he would have taken one of my legs right out. I believe the power of the blood of Jesus stopped that from happening.

The reality became larger as I went to the body shop, and they could not believe I was okay. My vehicle stayed in the shop for weeks, but I went home and slept in my own bed that night with zero injuries. Sometime later, I researched exactly how much weight I had been hit by. You see, the cab of the semi-truck weighed around 19,000 lbs. The flatbed trailer weighed about 12,000 lbs. He hit me 3 times, so I got hit by about 93,000 lbs. of weight that morning...yet I went home and slept in my own bed unharmed. You cannot explain that except it was only because of the tremendous power in the awesome blood of Jesus Christ. Yeah, God!

This all happened as I was still trying to get back on my legs, and God still has me here today to testify of His goodness! Thank you, Lord! I am so thankful that Heaven decided to warn me to wake up and pray. When He does that, it's important to obey as it could save someone's life or even your own life.

Broken-Down Jesus Girl
Touches the Heart
of a King

It is my hope that as you read this last story, that you will actually see beyond your brokenness. We have all been broken, some more than others it seems. I even had a prophecy by a famous prophet that I was a modern-day Job, like Job in the Bible.

The good news is we don't have to stay there. The reality of how God used me In such a time still impacts me and others today. Even in very difficult times, if you say yes to the One who holds you, you, too, can impact hearts on a deep level.

After my first ambulance ride and serious leg injury, I got a call from a friend one day. She excitedly announced that she had an event for us to live paint at. Her exact words were, "I got us a gig."

I told her, "I don't want a gig," and proceeded to remind her that I was not able to walk and was on crutches in case she had forgotten.

She proceeded to excitedly tell me that our mutual friend's uncles were coming to Canada. They were real, bloodline kings from Africa. Yes, they were actual royalty/monarchy from their nation. Our friend was monarchy by blood.

This friend was planning a conference and wanted us to be the live guest artists. We had both done live painting at conferences before, but this time was different as I literally felt like I could not do it due to my injury. I kindly thought that I would excuse myself due to not walking. I had several excuses why this simply would not work out. She would not take no for an answer.

You see, we artists think we should arrive with camels since we bring so much stuff like easels, canvases, paints of all kinds, drop cloths, etc. But then she stated matter-of-factly that she would be happy to carry ALL of my things. All I would have to do was attend and paint.

I honestly felt like the Lord Himself came and wiped out all my excuses. Somehow, it seemed that He wanted me to go. Hesitantly, I said, "Okay, I will come."

I still wrestled in my mind about the whole thing. Quite frankly, I was seriously hoping she would just find someone else. She did not.

The day came for the conference. Thankfully, I could drive, so we loaded up our vehicles and followed each other there.

When we got to the university where the event was being held, the real journey began. I hobbled a long way on crutches to reach a set of stairs. Managing to make it down about 7 or 8 stairs, we had to now walk down a never-ending hallway. I honestly do not think we could have parked further away. Remember, I was on crutches and likely mumbling under my breath, "Lord, what am I doing here? This is ridiculous!"

Upon arriving at the end of that long hallway, we came to what appeared to be about 20 to 30 stairs. These stairs led straight up to the ballroom where the conference would take place a few hours later.

Now, there was no way I could get up those stairs on crutches, and there was no elevator in sight. Nope, not even a "prince charming" was around who could come on his noble steed to pick me up and race me up that stairwell.

Here was the humbling moment, folks. I realized that the only way up those stairs was on my backside. Yes, you got that right, on my butt. (Sorry, folks, but there is just no classy way to describe this truth.) Thankfully, I prayed that no one would see me do this. I had done this hundreds of times at home but doing it there in public kind of took the cake. You can imagine my relief that there were no kings or reporters in sight. Somehow, I was protected by that as the whole scene was humiliating enough all by itself.

My girlfriend set us up, and we were ready to roll. The conference opened up. Suddenly, my girlfriend who was hosting the conference called me up to open in prayer. We had not discussed this prior, but the Word says to be ready in season, right? So, now I couldn't hide. Off I went to hobble up in front of the 3 kings. Then, I prayed and hobbled back to my easel.

The evening proceeded, and the Lord told me what to paint. Sometimes, He does that and other times I have had to just flow and paint and trust Him to show up and paint through me.

At the end of the evening, the oldest of the 3 kings walked over to my easel. He began to weep as he spoke to me. He said that he was 72 years old, and they had travelled the whole world and had never had anyone paint live for them before. Somehow, this touched him deeply.

I explained why I painted what I did. He wept some more. That was a precious moment, and it caught my attention.

The following day, we painted again. At the end of that day as my friend and other folks were packing and cleaning up after the conference, I was tired and felt useless. I recall going to sit on the floor at the back of the room, mentally preparing to go down all those stairs again.

I had a little chat with the Lord. It went like this: "Seriously, Lord? You took a broken-down Jesus girl like me and used me to touch the heart of a king?" I was in awe.

For all of us, I believe there is a life lesson here. Even in your most broken state, do not underestimate how God can use you to touch a life or many lives. The anointing is often strong in brokenness because then you cannot rely on yourself at all. The glory goes to Him alone. He is only asking that we be willing, that is all. Then, He can show up and show off. Your "yes" is no small thing to Him. Never put it past Him to wipe away all your excuses either.

Later that week, the mayor of the city was having breakfast with the kings. We were invited to an African Durbar dinner and dance with the kings, their queens, and their princesses, etc. They somehow reminded me of the Trinity with the older king, the middle king who loved to dance with his queen, and the younger king. The dancing king really enjoyed himself and smiled the whole time.

I had had a prophecy that my art would go places and shift the atmosphere, which I have heard testimonies of. One gal was healed of a deathly illness when I painted a bouquet, and we hung it over her bed. She also had dreams and visions open up that night. Well, the kings went home with some of our art. I heard a short while later that one of them got saved. Glory be to God!

"Ransomed Warrior"

Poem by Rhéa Dallaire
December 2, 2015

It is good to live with a ransomed, delivered, fearless, courageous, and enlarged heart. Think on the battles you've fought for, the battles you've won, the ones you are now being given from My own Son. Think on the long-lost dreams, hopes, and wishes you've brought to My Throne while doing the dishes.

For a time is coming upon the earth... I'm restoring and bringing these dreams back to birth. Can you see the graveyard covered in sand—lost, sunken armour being retrieved by My hand?

So, all is not lost. Get ready to run. Victories are being held for you by the hand of My Son. As chaos and disorder try to come into the land, your hearts have a role to play saying "NO" 'til the end. For the mighty name of "Brave Heart" was given but not just for a few. You see, the name "Brave Heart" was given to each of you.

So, pick up your armour. Ready or not, get back into battle and give it your best shot. Let courage arise in your most-deepest parts. So, get ready warriors. I'm enlarging your hearts.

The time is not here for worries or cares. Get ready, dear ones. Cast your cares in the air. You'll not grow mighty sitting on the sidelines. You're about to see life getting redefined.

If you've lived for yourself, you'll not have much to show. If you've lived sowing seeds, you'll see much start to grow. Start to grow here and there and spread through the land. If you live for My Son, you will see My right hand.

There are some who sit and wonder, "Oh, what's in it for me?" And sitting on their duff, they are as lonely as can be. But for those in alignment and for those who've decreed, the best days are yet to come. The Trinity agrees!

Summary

Heaven caught my attention to write. Eleven prophecies told me to write these stories out. I was told that these stories needed to be shared to give people hope.

We are living in uncertain times. I sense that I have gone through what many folks may go through now or in the future perhaps. So, if telling my story helps to bring God glory, that's great.

My heart's desire would be that you, the reader, would find courage in these pages. I pray that the words would go deep in your heart, and when you need faith for a miracle, you would know that they still exist today. I pray that you would hunger and thirst to know the God of the breakthrough on a deeper level.

Acts 26:22 in the Passion Bible (TPT) says, *"But in spite of all this, I have experienced the supernatural help of God up to this very moment..."* I can say that this is true!

As I have read and reread my manuscript, I, too, have been in awe of how Heaven kissed me and my earthly realm. So, never give up, keep hope on a rope, and keep faith on your plate as there are precious lives at stake! If God can take a broken-down Jesus girl and do it for me, He will do it for you too.

There are many great and wonderful days ahead for you and me. My hope is, if you even feel like your wings have been clipped or broken, that you, too, can learn to fly again. Trust me, you will!

May God bless you all!

Rhéa Hope

P.S. I've got my new wings and am ready to fly!

Manufactured by Amazon.ca
Bolton, ON